THE
DREAM
GIVER
for
Parents

BRUCE & DARLENE MARIE
WILKINSON

WITH ANDRIES CILLIERS

Multnomah® Publishers *Sisters, Oregon*

THE DREAM GIVER FOR PARENTS
published by Multnomah Publishers, Inc.
Based on *The Dream Giver* by Bruce Wilkinson
and David and Heather Kopp

© 2004 by Exponential, Inc.
International Standard Book Number: 1-59052-455-1

Published in South Africa by Lux Verbi.BM

Unless otherwise indicated, Scripture quotations are from:
The Holy Bible, New King James Version © 1984 by Thomas Nelson, Inc.
Other Scripture quotations are from:
The Holy Bible, New International Version (NIV) © 1973, 1984 by International Bible
Society, used by permission of Zondervan Publishing House

Multnomah is a trademark of Multnomah Publishers, Inc.,
and is registered in the U.S. Patent and Trademark Office.
The colophon is a trademark of Multnomah Publishers, Inc.

Printed in the United States of America

For information:
MULTNOMAH PUBLISHERS, INC. · P. O. BOX 1720 · SISTERS, OR 97759

Library of Congress Cataloging-in-Publication Data

Wilkinson, Bruce.
    The dream giver for parents / Bruce Wilkinson and Darlene Marie
Wilkinson ; with Andres Cilliers.
        p. cm.
    Includes bibliographical references.
    ISBN 1-59052-455-1
    1. Parents—Religious life. 2. Parenting—Religious aspects—
Christianity I. Wilkinson, Darlene. II. Cilliers, Andres. III.
Wilkinson, Bruce Dream giver. IV. Title.
    BV4529.W556 2004
    248.8'45—dc22
                                            2004015518

05 06 07 08 09—10 9 8 7 6 5 4 3 2

CONTENTS

PART I

A PARABLE FOR PARENTS

❧

PART II

SEVEN SECRETS FOR RAISING A DREAMER

PREFACE

*D*o you believe that every child is born with a Dream
for his or her life? And that you were born with one, too?
No matter where we travel or who we talk to, we have yet
to find one person who *doesn't* have a Dream. He may not
be able to describe it. He may have buried it deep in some
corner of his heart. He may no longer believe in it.

But it's there.

All of us have a sense of wanting to "do something
meaningful" with our lives. We call this universal and
powerful longing a Big Dream. And, like the genetic code
that describes one's unique passions and abilities, your
child's Big Dream has been woven into his or her being
from before birth—therefore it never is quite like
someone else's Dream. In fact, your child's unique
makeup points toward his or her Dream. And as a parent
it is your privilege to help your child discover and shape
his or her Dream.

In my book *The Dream Giver,* I talked about Dreams and the Giver of our Dreams, as well as the obstacles we encounter on our Journey pursuing our Dreams. Our prayer is that *The Dream Giver* will help you discover and live *your* unique Dream (it never is too late for that!). This book, *The Dream Giver for Parents,* is a practical guide for inspiring and supporting *your children* on their Dream Journey. Like *The Dream Giver,* it is made up of two sections. Part I is a customized modern-day parable about parents settled in the Land of Familiar who learn to accept and actively support their children's burning desire to pursue their Big Dreams. We meet Mr. and Mrs. Ordinary Sr., who have a difficult time when their son, Ordinary, sets out on his Journey, as well as the Comforts, whose daughter is just discovering her Dream. This story will introduce you to the big ideas we want to talk about in part II, "Seven Secrets for Raising a Dreamer," where we share with you seven secrets for guiding your children to discover and pursue their Dreams.

Dreamers soon learn that every Dream Journey is clogged with Dream-threatening obstacles. That is why it is so important for Big Dreamers to have great perseverance. The more you expose your children to information and experiences relating to their interests and talents, the better equipped they will be for their Journey, and the less likely they will be to abandon their Dreams. And the more you rely on the Dream Giver for guidance and inspiration, the better they will understand that God is shaping their Dreams to fit in with His Big Dream for the world.

So we'd like to ask you: Have you noticed the beginnings of a Big Dream in your child, but maybe it has gotten lost along the way? Or is he or she experiencing one setback after another? Or do you feel as if God has completely forgotten to give your child a Big Dream? Perhaps your own Dream didn't work out, and you want to spare your child that heartache by not mentioning Big Dreams at all.

May this book help you become a Dreamer again— enjoying your child's Dreams as well as your own. May it convince you that the Dreams God placed in your child's heart (and in your own heart) fit in with His purpose for you. And may it inspire you and your child to actively pursue your Dreams.

The world is waiting—and so is the Dream Giver!

Warmly,

Bruce and Darlene Marie Wilkinson

Johannesburg, South Africa

PART I

A Parable for Parents

God created you for a higher purpose.
This is the most important journey of your life,
pursuing your God-given purpose.
BRUCE WILKINSON

THE DREAM GIVER

*I*n the Land of Familiar, not far from here, lived Mom and Dad and their only son, Ordinary. He had become notorious in Familiar for daring to leave in search of what he called his Big Dream.

"We always knew there was something wrong with him," people would say when Ordinary's parents were out of earshot. But to their faces they said, "It must be. . .*interesting* to have such a *special* child!"

Mom was having a hard time because of her son. On the day she first held little Ordinary in her arms, she said: "Ordie, my sweetie, Mommy promises to always keep you safe." Now she didn't even know where he was. The last time she had seen him, he was rowing in a small boat across the Wide Waters bordering the extreme ends of Familiar. Since then, she hadn't heard from him. He had said that he was on his way to some unknown Land of Promise. However, Mom had no peace of mind. What if this road led straight to the WasteLand—that desolate region about which one heard only the most horrid tales?

"To him it might be a Dream," she would complain to Dad, "but to me it is one endless nightmare. And it's all your fault. Dreaming runs on *your* side of the family." She wasn't entirely mistaken. In his youth, Dad had had a Dream, too, but he had buried it so deeply that he could hardly remember what it was. He didn't have the courage to leave Familiar and embark on the dangerous quest for his Dream.

"The moment Ordie mentioned this Dream thing, you became excited," Mom had upbraided Dad when Ordinary announced he was leaving. "You could have talked him out of it. But no-o-o, you had to start dreaming along with him. At your age, it's just ridiculous!"

"If a parent can't dream along with his child," Dad had answered, "how will that child ever come to believe in his Dreams? I wish *my* dad had been enthusiastic about my Dreams."

Mom had snorted and set out after Ordinary to stop him. However, when she returned alone with the news that Ordinary was determined to pursue his Dream, she had changed her tune. "This Dream thing still is a bit of a mystery to me," she said. "But I do know now that my son had to get into that little boat and cross the Wide Waters. He just *has* to pursue his Dream."

Since then, Mom had been torn by conflicting emotions. She believed her Ordie had done the right thing, but she was haunted by the fact that her son was out there in the Unknown. When others in Familiar implied that Ordinary had lost his mind, she jumped to his defense. But in quiet moments, she regretted that Ordinary had ever become involved in Dreams.

"*I* would have refused to let him go," said her best friend, Mollycoddle Mom. "If *my* child had entertained any such notion, I would have stopped her, even if I had to scream or cry or fake a heart attack. No daughter of mine is leaving Familiar. It's pure madness!"

Mom tried to change the subject. "And how *is* Little Molly? Is she still polishing teaspoons for Familiar Kitchenware? Or is it forks?" But as soon as Mollycoddle Mom left, she threw herself on the bed, crying over Ordinary.

❧

That's where Dad found Mom when he arrived home from his Usual Job. He sat down beside her on the bed and put his arms around her.

"I don't get this Dream thing!" Mom sobbed. "Explain it to me—after all, you were afflicted by Dreams when you were young, weren't you?"

Dad was quiet for a moment. Then he replied, "I think you also have a Dream."

"Me? Whatever gave you that idea? I am an ordinary, respectable citizen of Familiar. You won't catch me getting into little boats, rowing off while my poor mother stands crying on the shore!"

But Dad wouldn't be put off that easily. "Just think," he said. "What made you set out after Ordinary to try and stop him?"

"I wanted to be a good mother," Mom murmured. "I'm concerned about my child's safety."

"Exactly!" Dad said. "That's a Dream, too, you know. We are living our Dreams when we become what we were born to be—when we're able to say, 'I am happy when I'm like this.' Tell me, have you ever found a long white feather?"

Mom sat bolt upright. "Why?"

"Well, when I discovered my Dream as a young man, I found such a white feather. But as time passed and I didn't do anything about it, my feather turned to dust. Ordinary also found a feather along with his Dream, but he used his for keeping his Dream Journal. . .because he had discovered that he had no choice but to pursue his Dream. The white feather is a sign that you did not invent your Dream yourself—that it comes from the Dream Giver."

"I did find a white feather—on the day Ordinary was born," Mom mused. "I've never understood what it meant. You know, I've never paid much attention to this Dream Giver talk. Yet I kept the feather. It should be somewhere in one of Ordie's albums."

She jumped up to go look for it. And there it was— slightly discolored and tattered—still lying between the pages of the album. She took it out and gently stroked the photos of little Ordinary. "I used to tickle him with this when he was little," she remembered.

"Then his dreaming streak is *your* fault." Dad said, laughing. "I should have guessed!"

"But this doesn't make sense. *My* Dream definitely is to be a good mother and keep Ordie safe. But *his* Dream is to set out and expose himself to who knows what kinds of danger. Our Dreams are mutually exclusive!"

"Perhaps you don't really understand your Dream," Dad said. "It *is* about being a good mother to Ordinary, that's clear. And when he was young, this meant cuddling him and looking out for his safety. But as he grew up, your Dream should have grown with him."

"Are you saying that my Dream of keeping him safe was not big enough for him?" asked Mom.

"No, not big enough for *you!*" answered Dad excitedly. "Yes, I see it now: When you allowed Ordinary to row away from you in pursuit of his Dream, you were actually fulfilling your Dream, too. You were still being a good mother. It's just that your Dream had grown bigger. It's a much bigger Dream to let your children go than to cling to them. That's a Dream big enough for a woman like you!"

"But if that's true, why am I suffering so much?" Mom wondered.

"Because nothing worthwhile comes easy. A Dream that comes true too easily doesn't really bring any meaning into a person's life. Dreaming of keeping your children dependent is not worth much. But dreaming of sending them out into the world to pursue their Dreams? That's a Big Dream in itself!"

"Now don't you start preaching at me," laughed Mom. "I've decided to use this white feather for writing about my Dream and about Ordinary and how hard it is not knowing where he is."

Suddenly, the feather in her hands was transformed— it became pure white and brand new, as if she had just received it.

∾

"Looking back," Mom wrote with the white feather in her new Dream Journal, "I realize that Ordinary has always been on his way to Big Things. I remember him building a whole city in the mud in our garden when he was very small."

"'Look, Mom,' he said, 'it's a place where everyone can live well, a much better place than the Land of Familiar.' And I joined him in all this! It never occurred to me that I was sharing his Dream. Perhaps that's a good thing. . ."

She was remembering how Mollycoddle Mom used to remark disapprovingly, "No child of mine will ever play in the mud like that—" when there was a knock at the door. It was Mollycoddle Mom, her face red with crying.

"I just don't know what to do anymore," she sobbed as she collapsed onto Dad's recliner. "Little Molly won't eat. She doesn't want to go anywhere or do anything. She says she hates her life; she just wants to curl up and die."

Mollycoddle Mom blew her nose. "I tried to comfort her, reminding her of her comfortable job. But then she burst out that if she never saw another knife in her life, it wouldn't be too soon."

It was knives she polished, Mom remembered then. Little Molly was Assistant Knife Polisher. But now she seemed to have become dissatisfied.

"And you know Difficult Dad." Mollycoddle Mom burst into tears again. "All my life I have had to protect Little Molly from him. He says the child needs a firm hand and that he'll cut her off if she doesn't stop her nonsense. So I thought I might have a talk with you because you have a problem child, too, and you. . ."

"He's no problem child," Mom snapped back. "I have a Dreamer child, and I have come to understand only lately that following one's Dream is actually what we all should be doing. Perhaps that is Little Molly's problem— she doesn't like what she's doing. Have you ever tried talking to her about what she would like to do? Maybe that job Difficult Dad arranged for her doesn't suit her. If she could do what she loves, she might get a taste for life again. Perhaps she has a Dream of her own?"

"I don't think it's anything *that* serious," Mollycoddle Mom said anxiously. "And what's the point of asking her what she wants to do? For goodness' sake, we're her parents. If we don't know what's best for her, then who does? Polishing knives is honest work."

Mom suddenly had an idea. "Would you like to read this?" She held up her Dream Journal. "I actually didn't intend for anyone to read it, but perhaps it will help you." She pressed the Journal into Mollycoddle Mom's hands.

No one spoke for quite a while as she sat reading. At last, Mollycoddle Mom broke the silence.

"I think I know what I have to do. I'll have to have a talk with Little Molly about what she really wants. Just like you, I want to be a good mother, but I don't always know how."

"You'll learn along the way," Mom assured her. "That's what we all have to do."

❧

The following afternoon, Mom was writing in her Dream Journal when Mollycoddle Mom appeared once more at the front door. This time Little Molly was with her.

"So much for Dreams!" Mollycoddle Mom burst out. "Do you know what the child wants to do? She wants to draw."

"And...?"

"You don't understand! She doesn't want to draw useful things, like new designs for knives. She wants to draw...other people's Dreams. She has a white feather, just like yours and Ordinary's, and she thinks she could help people understand their Dream if she talked to them about it and then drew it for them. She thinks if people had a clear picture of their Dreams, they would be more successful at living them."

"Sounds like a wonderful Dream to me!" Mom smiled. Little Molly shyly drew closer to her.

"But there is no work in the Land of Familiar for

Dream Draftsmen!" sobbed Mollycoddle Mom. "She'll never make a living! And what will Difficult Dad say? He hates 'silly pictures' and hates Dreams, and now his daughter wants to follow a career in both!"

"Little Molly is a big girl," Mom said, although the tearful girl next to her didn't look it just then. "She can decide for herself. If she wants to be a Dream Draftsman, we have to help her."

"I know of a Dream Draftsman who lives here," Little Molly offered timidly. "Perhaps I could go see him. . ."

"I'll take you there. . ." said Mom.

"I'm coming with you. We will see. . ." said Mollycoddle Mom.

∾

The Dream Draftsman lived on a small street in a poorer part of Familiar. His little house was filled with pictures.

"How did you think up all of this?" asked Mollycoddle Mom, stunned.

"I don't think up anything," explained the Dream Draftsman. "Dreams are created by the Dream Giver, who puts them into the right people's hearts. He gave me the gift of helping people see what Dreams He has for them. They understand their Dreams better if they have a picture of what they look like."

He looked at Mom. "You're Ordinary's mother, aren't you?" He rummaged around and took out a few pictures. "Ordinary asked me to draw his Dream before he went

away. He left this one here because he hoped you or his
father would one day like to see it."

The first picture was of little Ordie just as she
remembered him—in the mud, his Dream City in front
of him. Mom was speechless.

"I drew two more after Ordinary left. I don't
understand why the Dream Giver had me draw these, too,
but perhaps it was because you will need them." The
second picture shocked Mom. It showed Ordinary
walking around a rundown city, surrounded by thin,
hungry-looking children.

"Yuck," said Mollycoddle Mom. "Doesn't look like
much of a Dream Picture to me."

"But see how happy he looks?" exclaimed Little Molly.
"As if he's exactly where he needs to be! This is the most
beautiful picture I've ever seen."

Mom took another look. It was true. She had never
seen Ordinary looking so happy. Then she saw the third
picture. Ordinary was standing on the wall of a beautiful
city. Around him smiling children were playing. "This is
possible," explained the Dream Draftsman, "if Ordinary
follows his Dream."

"I wish I could draw like that," said Little Molly.

The Dream Draftsman gave her a long look. Then he
said, "You will." He turned to Mollycoddle Mom.
"And. . .you will too."

Mollycoddle Mom blushed flaming red. "I did dream
a bit, a long time ago, but. . ."

"Mother!" accused Little Molly with a laugh. "You never said a thing!"

The two began talking excitedly to the Dream Draftsman. Mom stood there, hugging Ordinary's three Dream Pictures. Nobody noticed her leave and take the pictures with her.

∾

Back home, Mom put the Dream Pictures away with the white feather and her Dream Journal. Then she heard the front door open. She walked quickly to the door. It was Dad, and he had a stranger with him. The man was emaciated and looked sickly. His eyes were dull and his hands shook.

Dad put an arm around Mom's shoulders. "Darling," he said, "this is Turnabout. I am afraid he has some very bad news for us."

"Ordinary?" asked Mom.

Turnabout nodded, but did not look her in the eye.

"He can't be dead, I know he isn't dead!" cried Mom. "I would have known. . . "

"When I saw him last in the WasteLand," murmured Turnabout, "he was thin, and his clothing was ragged, but he was alive."

"The WasteLand?" cried Mom. "But he was heading for the Land of Promise!"

"The Land of Promise?" Turnabout laughed gruffly.

"Yes, didn't we all believe that old story? take it from me—I, too, entered the WasteLand hoping to reach the Land of Promise. There is no such place! That's one of the reasons I turned back."

"If the Land of Promise doesn't exist, where is Ordinary now?" Dad wondered.

"When I last saw him, he was on his way to the Valley of Giants," replied Turnabout. "No one can overcome the Giants. I've seen with my own eyes how they kill Dreamers who are trying to defeat them on their way to the Land of Promise."

"But what about the Dream Giver?" Mom asked. "Isn't He supposed to help Dreamers overcome the Giants?"

"The Dream Giver. . . ?" Turnabout's voice dropped. "I also used to believe in Him. But He did not relieve my suffering in the WasteLand or show me a shortcut out of there or remove the Giants from my path. I sometimes think He doesn't care what happens to us on the road *He* told us to take! Perhaps He doesn't even exist."

"But you did say that Ordinary was still alive," Mom argued. "There's still hope!"

"No. I'm so sorry," whispered Turnabout, so softly that she could hardly hear him. "I saw the Giants and I saw Ordinary. I can't imagine him having any chance of surviving the Valley of Giants."

"But he was still alive!" Mom insisted.

That evening, Dad and Mom sat talking in the dusky living room. "It's all my fault," he said. "I never learn. I knew dreaming was dangerous—that's why *I* didn't go through with it. But then I go and encourage my son to embark on a crazy journey to follow his Dream. I never should have trusted the Dream Giver."

Mom said nothing. She sat paging through Ordinary's album, longing for those little-boy arms around her neck. She felt like nothing she could say would make any difference. Suddenly she remembered the Dream Pictures. She went to get them and showed them to Dad, telling him what the Dream Draftsman said.

Dad sat looking at the pictures for a long time. At last he said, "They're only pictures. They're not reality. The reality is that I allowed my child to suffer through the WasteLand and indirectly sent him on an impossible mission in the Valley of Giants. Pictures are just pictures. But the truth is that I have cost Ordinary his life."

"I don't know. These pictures give me hope," Mom said. "I believe that the Dream Giver gave the Dream Draftsman this picture to draw so we would know that Ordinary will reach the Land of Promise. I trust the Dream Giver. Before He was nothing more than a name to me, but I have learned something through all of this. I've learned that He really *is* with us. And I believe He is with Ordinary, too. We can't be there, but He is."

"Just pictures and empty talk!" muttered Dad.

"I know exactly what I'm going to do. I'm going to write in my Dream Journal, 'I put Ordinary in Your hands, Dream Giver. Do with him as You think best,'" said Mom. Then she began to cry.

Suddenly there was a bright light in the living room, shining around them and through them. A voice said, "I am with you."

Mom and Dad sank to their knees. Dad stammered, "Oh, Dream Giver, I'm so sorry that I—"

"I understand," said the Dream Giver. "It has been very hard for you, letting go of Ordinary. But before he was yours, he was Mine. And he remains in My hands, not yours."

"Is he safe?" Mom's heart stood still.

"That is not for you to know right now. Ordinary's life story is between him and Me. I want to talk to you about your lives. But if you don't trust Me, it will be of no use."

"We're trying, but it's difficult!" exclaimed Dad.

"I know, but be patient. Be still and wait."

They sat quietly and waited. And waited. And waited.

The light began to fade, but they kept on waiting. Eventually the room was pitch black, and still they waited. *There is nothing else for us to do,* they thought. *We'll just have to be patient.*

∾

It became a very long wait. Mom and Dad received no news from Ordinary. And there wasn't a single word from

the Dream Giver either. All they had to hold on to was
the memory of his words, *Be still and wait.* That, and the
three Dream Pictures.

One day Mollycoddle Mom popped in. "You're not
going to believe this," she said, breathless with
excitement. "Little Molly is drawing like a dream! And
she is so happy!" She hesitated for a moment and then
took a picture from a large file she was carrying. "And I
don't draw too badly either."

Mom looked at the drawing. The lines still were a bit
shaky, but it really wasn't too bad. What surprised her
most was the subject of the picture. Mollycoddle Mom
had drawn Difficult Dad with arms outstretched. One
hand was beckoning, as if inviting intimacy, while the
other was pushing away.

"I realized what Difficult Dad is really like," explained
Mollycoddle Mom. "His Dream is actually to love people,
but he's too afraid to let anyone come near him." She
laughed. "Now I must find the courage to show him this
picture! He still hasn't made peace with our 'silly
pictures'!"

Mom stroked the drawing absentmindedly, thinking
again of Ordinary and his pictures. "I wish I knew what
happens to Dreams," she said.

But Mollycoddle Mom wasn't listening. "And this is
Little Molly's. It's far better than mine."

Little Molly's Dream Picture showed Ordinary
standing on a rock. In front of him was darkness, but he
was looking back, his face to the light. A little ways behind

him, Little Molly herself was standing, her eyes on Ordinary's face. "You realize what this means, of course," Mollycoddle Mom was saying. "She wants to follow him as soon as she has learned to draw well. She says she just knows that where Ordinary now finds himself, they need a Dream Draftsman."

"But we don't know where he is!" Mom began to cry. "We don't even know if he's still alive. I told Dad that I trust the Dream Giver, but sometimes I'm not so sure."

"Let me tell you something," Mollycoddle Mom answered, as she hugged Mom. "I don't know if Ordinary is still alive. But one thing I do know is that almost everything I know about being a good mother I learned from you. You made sure that we went to see the Dream Draftsman. And Little Molly says Ordinary was the first to show her that people can live their Dreams. I think the Dream Giver has given us you two as examples so that we could see what the road ahead looks like. If I had to draw a Dream Picture of you, it would show you comforting me someday because I didn't know where Little Molly was right then."

At first Mom said nothing. Then she dried her tears and said, "You know what? I think you've just given me back my Dream! Maybe the Dream Giver wants to show me that I can give other people the same love and care I gave Ordinary. So many people out there are hurt or broken and are in need of a little safety and security, and that's something I can do very well—make people feel safe!"

෧

That evening Dad arrived home excited and relieved, holding a letter from Ordinary—sent from the Land of Promise! He and Mom read it together, over and over again:

My dearest Mom and Dad,

I am writing to you after a very long journey. I made it! I'm living in the Land of Promise now, watching my Big Dream come true all around me. And to think it all began with sticks and mud, when I was just a little boy!

I have realized that every single person has a Dream—and that it never is too late to pursue it. I know you think your Dream has died, Dad, but a Big Dream from the Dream Giver never dies. Your Dream is here somewhere, just waiting for you to start living it. And if you don't pursue it, something important might never happen.

As you will see, Dad, I'm sending you my feather. It will help you on the long road that lies ahead. It will lead you straight to a miracle that has your name on it! The same goes for Mom, who, of course, also has a Big Dream.

I can't wait to see you both again here in the Land of Promise.

I miss you!

All my love,

Your son, Ordinary

"Seems like we'd better start packing," said Dad.

"Sure, but let's wait a while." Mom smiled. "There's someone I want to invite along, but she isn't quite ready for the journey."

Mom began making plans to persuade Difficult Dad to allow Little Molly to embark upon her Dream Journey. *Who knows,* Mom thought, *perhaps when Ordinary and Little Molly meet again. . ."*

And she saw a new Dream taking shape.

PART II

SEVEN SECRETS
FOR
RAISING A DREAMER

Dare to let your children dream of *changing the world.*

Raise them with Dreams that will bring *meaning* into their lives.

Explore all the life-areas *they are good at or that excite them*—clear indicators of the made-to-fit Dreams God put into their hearts.

Affirm your own belief in your children's Dreams by exposing them to all the available *information and experiences* that will help them define their Dreams.

Make use of every opportunity to help them learn from *role models*—positive *and* negative.

Encourage your children to rely on the Dream Giver as the *only Guide* who will show them how to shape their Dreams to fit in with God's Big Dream for the world.

Remind them that following your dreams demands *perseverance,* tenacity, and creative problem solving.

SECRET NUMBER 1:
DARE

DARE to let your children dream
of changing the world.

Teach your child that things can change;
the same child whose thoughts you influence
in this way eventually will change the world.
BRUCE WILKINSON

❧

Of all the wonderful things my parents taught me,
one stands out above all else: they believed everyone
could make a difference in the world.
They taught me I could choose to live in such a way
that after my death people could say the world
was a better place because I had been there.
GERALD G. JAMPOLSKY,
ONE PERSON CAN MAKE A DIFFERENCE

∞

It is unthinkable that one could be born, marry,
have children and die without having done something—
however small—to change the world for the better.
HARRY OPPENHEIMER

*S*he has reached her thirties, but she is still struggling
for direction. Life plainly is getting her down. There are
dark rings under her eyes. She looks tired. Once you get
her talking, her bitterness becomes evident: "My father
always told me I was nothing and would never amount to
anything. And now I believe it, too."

Consider this case: A young learner experiences one
setback after another. He used to be an excellent athlete,
but injuries from a car accident left him out of action for
six months. Then just when he was able to start practicing
again, he broke his leg. The doctors said he could consider
sports only after another six months. But by then he
almost would have finished school! Although this was a
huge disappointment, he insists, "I will run again." How
could he be so full of hope, so certain? "My mother gave
me new running shoes for my birthday. If she believes I
will run again, then so do I."

One parent crushed any Dreams his daughter might
have had; the other affirmed her son's Dream. In *The
Dream Giver,* I emphasize some truths about people and
their Dreams:

❦ Everyone has a Dream.

❦ You do not have to create your Dream yourself.

❦ Every person's Dream is unique and important.

❦ Dreams are meant to be lived.

Don't you want to guard these truths for your child? Do you remember the day your child was born? You just knew God had a special plan for that little person. This is your sense that God builds a Life Dream into each one of us to become what we were meant to be.

I don't know how you feel about your child today. Perhaps you're excited about his sports achievements or her academic success. Perhaps you're worried about wrong friends or bad habits. Maybe you feel that you don't know your child anymore. The years might have dimmed your memories of that first moment you held your child.

Well, I challenge you today to remind yourself:

❦ This child has a Dream.

❦ It isn't up to me or my child to create a Dream for him or her, for our Dreams come from God. But my child must discover his or her Dream.

❦ The Dream that the Dream Giver has placed in my child's heart is as unique as his or her fingerprints.

❦ My child was born to live this Dream.

Now ask yourself this: What part do I play in my children's Dreams? Am I the kind of parent who crushes Dreams—or do I dream along with them about the place

God has prepared for them in His Big Dream for the
world?

JOSEPH

Joseph is certainly the best-known Dreamer in the Bible.
He discovered his Dream when he still was very young,
but it was only after many setbacks that it was finally
realized. And only when his Dream had become reality
did Joseph fully understand what it actually meant...

Imagine a newspaper reporter interviewing Joseph,
Egypt's most successful politician and economist—the
man who single-handedly averted famine in the country
and indeed the whole region. This reporter probably
would have asked, "What would you say is the secret of
your success?"

I picture Joseph answering, "Well, you see, I had this
Dream... In fact, I have been a Dreamer since I was a
small boy." After thinking it over a little, he might have
added, "Actually, the whole story began *before* my first
Dream—on the day when my father gave me that
stunning robe..."

We know the whole story as the Bible tells it in
Genesis 37–47. Being the first son of Jacob's beloved wife,
Rachel, Joseph was his father's favorite. His half-brothers,
however, had very little time for him (who likes a Daddy's
boy?). The fact that he tattled to Jacob about all their
misdeeds didn't help (who likes a tattletale?).

This was no happy family. In fact, undercurrents of jealousy and discord ran throughout. We can't whitewash the unfair way Jacob treated his other sons or Joseph's irritating tales. However, this also is the story of a father who loved his son and gave him a richly decorated robe. This robe made Joseph stand out among his brothers, indicating that he was meant to be a leader. Even before Joseph himself had a Dream about being a leader, his father had recognized this quality in him. It's almost as if Jacob was preparing his son to pursue his Dream.

In this respect, Jacob made no mistake. Because he loved Joseph so well, he had a notion of the Dream his son was meant to live, which is why he gave him a Dreamcoat: to prepare him for this Dream. Jacob's big mistake was that he did not love his other children as much.

LOVE AND DREAMS

Children whose Dreams are overlooked often go astray. One thing is certain: *Without love, parents are incapable of teaching their children how to discover and live their Dreams.* Instead, one or more of the following might happen:

- You know about your child's Dreams, but are unable to do anything about it.
- You make your child feel like a failure if he or she doesn't succeed in living these Dreams.

❧ You ignore your child's Dreams or even crush them.
❧ You force your child unfeelingly toward making his or her Dreams come true.
❧ You impose your own Dreams on your child.

Most parents surely would answer, "Of course I love my child!" But the Bible reminds us that we need more than natural parental love: Love should be complemented by knowledge and depth of insight so that we may be able to discern what is best (Philippians 1:9–10). Sometimes the lyrics of the old song also apply to parents, "We loved not too wisely..." *Wise* love is what parents who want to make their children Dreamers need.

The 1996 film *Shine* tells the story of Australian concert pianist David Helfgott, who was a child prodigy. Unfortunately, he grew up in a dysfunctional family, which almost destroyed his Dream of an international career as a musician. David's father, Peter, a Jew who lived during the Nazi terror, lost almost his entire family.

Even though he survived the Holocaust, Peter was emotionally damaged in the process. He was paranoid about losing his family again, just like when he was a child. He loved his wife and children, especially the gifted young David, with a sincere but *distorted* love. He tried binding his family to him by ruling them with an iron fist. Their yard was even enclosed by barbed wire and a gate to which only he had the keys!

David's sensitive young life was further complicated by his father's obsession with his talented son winning every competition, no matter what the emotional cost, while absolutely refusing to let David compete internationally. Peter was so determined to stay in control of David's Dream that he steadily denied David wonderful opportunities by forbidding him to accept scholarship study in America and London.

In spite of his love for his son, Peter Helfgott did not have the insight to realize that he was stifling his son's dream. When David rebelled at age nineteen and decided to go overseas, his father cut him off completely. His demoralizing childhood, being rejected by his father, and the emotional strain of trying to prove himself as a pianist finally resulted in David suffering a complete breakdown. He spent the next ten years as a broken man in one psychiatric institution after another, his talent lying dormant and his name forgotten. Without the love and encouragement of an exceptional woman, who accepted David's broken spirit and eccentric nature and helped him rebuild his Dream, David Helfgott never would have been able to "shine" again and inspire the world with his phenomenal talent.

So what does wise parental love look like? In the first place, wise love is willing to get to know, understand, and enjoy every child for the unique person he or she is. Be prepared to *spend time* with them peacefully, without making them feel that they have to do something to impress you or that they are making inroads on your valuable time.

I am reminded of the little boy who one day asked his

father, an extremely busy businessman, how much he earned per hour. When the father at last gave his son a moment's attention, it was only to reply with irritation: "Really, what would you understand of such things?" When the boy timidly pressed him for an answer, he barked, "Let's say $35 an hour."

Over the next few days the child offered to clean the swimming pool, mow the lawns, and do all sorts of other chores for spending money. He even mowed the neighbors' lawns and washed their cars. He began delivering newspapers, too, and one morning, on his way out for his delivery round, he ran into his father, who also was up at dawn and on his way to work. The boy grabbed the opportunity to ask his father to wait a minute—he wanted to fetch something important from his room to show him. Impatiently, the father answered, "Just make it quick! I'm in a hurry!"

The child came running back to the already moving car. "Here's the $35 I've earned so far, Dad. Please, may I buy an hour of your time this evening?"

Wise love will convey this message to a child: "You are so important to me that I just want to spend some time with you. To be with you is a pleasure. That's why I have time for you." Darlene Marie remembers how we came to understand this with our own children:

I had been asking the Lord for creative ways to really express love to our son and daughter, who were four and five years old. One morning they

SEVEN SECRETS FOR RAISING A DREAMER 39

came running into the kitchen. David was bubbling over with excitement about something he and his sister, Jennifer, had been doing.

As he talked, I continued preparing their breakfast, nodding my head and adding an occasional, "How exciting!"

After several minutes, David abruptly stopped talking and accused me, "Mommy, you aren't listening to me!"

Turning around and facing them, I replied in a defensive tone, "Of course I am. I have heard every word."

He let out a deep sigh before pointing out sadly, "But your face is not listening!"

It wasn't enough to lend them my ear; they wanted my undivided attention. They wanted me to be excited along with them. Bruce and I began to understand that giving eye contact and genuinely "listening with our faces" made our children feel loved and important.

DREAM WITH YOUR CHILD

So you love your children with all the wisdom you can muster. You listen to them and have gained some indication of the Dreams that the Dream Giver has woven into their beings. Now you are ready to start dreaming with them.

But it is right here where we encounter one of our

biggest problems with our children's Dreams: *They make us uneasy.*

Initially, Jacob was so excited about Joseph's leadership potential that he had a Dreamcoat made for him. And when Joseph had his first Dream of being a leader, Jacob must have told himself, *There it is! I knew he had it in him!* But the second Dream Jacob found unsettling. In the first Dream, Joseph saw only his brothers' sheaves bow before him. But in the second Dream, it seemed as if Jacob himself would have to bow before his son. This was too much for the old father: "What is this dream you had?" he rebuked Joseph. "Will your mother and I and your brothers actually come and bow down to the ground before you?" (Genesis 37:9–10, NIV).

"What is this Dream you have?" This is the kind of serious, even frightening, reaction children often get from their parents and other adults. This is our way of warning them that such Dreams can upset the whole applecart. But we forget that playing around and experimenting—also with our Dreams—is part of being young. Joseph certainly did not understand his Dream clearly, but later on, in God's time, he would discover what his Dream really meant (see Genesis 45:5).

Often we approach our children's Dreams with a touch of negativity that we confuse with realism. Perhaps we have seen some of our own Dreams reduced to ashes. Perhaps we want to spare our children the pain of seeing their Dreams shattered, or help our families avoid the stress of misconceived dreaming. The problem with such "reality checks" is this: We risk crushing our children's Dreams even before they have had a chance to start dreaming.

The well-known story of Monty Roberts, the famous American horse breeder, illustrates how adults—mostly with the best of intentions—are in danger of crushing a child's Dream by being "realistic."

As a young boy, Monty wrote an enthusiastic school essay about his Big Dream of owning a stud farm, describing in minute detail what his farmhouse, the stables, and the training circuit would look like.

Monty got an F. He didn't come from a rich family, did he? his teacher said. Where was he going to find the huge sums of money for this ambitious project? No, Monty should write about a realistic goal; then the teacher would reconsider his grade.

Fortunately, Monty was not about to let anyone crush his Dream. He replied, "Sir, you keep your F and I'll keep my Dream."

Today Monty Roberts lives on exactly the kind of thriving stud farm he dreamed of as a child.[1]

When your children build an early Dream world of modeling clay or mud, the best thing you can do is to become a child again and join them. Then a stone can become a car and a couple of sticks a bridge. As they grow older, it is crucial to continue entering their Dream worlds by sharing their fantasies. While playing and dreaming together, you are sure to discover how they fit into the Dream Giver's Big Dream. Along the way, your children will discover that there indeed are some dreams they must abandon as unrealistic. But you might just as well discover that *your* idea of what is realistic must change to meet God's idea of what is possible!

The rest of this book is devoted to the many ways you can dream with your child—and how to discover the ultimate goal of our Dreams. This goal is nothing less than God's Big Purpose. He wants to change the world, and He gives us Dreams so that each one of us can play a unique role in this great transformation!

SECRET NUMBER 2:
RAISE

RAISE your children with Dreams
that will bring meaning into their lives.

*The secret of a happy life is to live for
a dream that is bigger than you are.*
MICHEL DE MONTAIGNE

❧

*Teach your children not to be afraid of life.
If you believe that life has meaning, your children will believe it,
too—and your believing this will help make it true.*
HENRY JAMES

❧

If you can do something, or dream that you will, make a start.
Some overconfidence is necessary to make one's dreams come true.
If you think you can do something, do it now.
And if you already are performing well, try doing better.
JOHANN WOLFGANG VON GOETHE

❧

At the fork in the way, I chose the road less traveled.
It made all the difference in the world.
ROBERT FROST

From his early years, he had nurtured a Dream. He wanted to be very rich. "When I hit forty, I want to retire and live the good life," he always said. And at forty his Dream came true. He retired at the coast. But within a few short months he reached a crisis point. He absolutely hated his new life. "The mistake I made," he said later, "was that I dreamed too big and fulfilled my Dream too soon. There was nothing left to make life worthwhile."

Actually, that was not where his mistake lay. The real problem was that he hadn't dreamed big *enough*. What he mistook for his Dream was too insignificant to give *meaning* to his life. His true Dream, the one the Dream Giver meant him to have, was much more than retiring at forty.

It is not enough to dream with your children about

instant happiness. Reach for Dreams that will bring meaning into their lives *in the long run.*

WILL ANY DREAM DO?

Andrew Lloyd Webber and Tim Rice wrote a musical about Joseph of the Bible, the well-known *Joseph and the Amazing Technicolor Dreamcoat.* One of the hit songs from this musical is "Any Dream Will Do." As long as you do have a Dream, so the song goes, it doesn't matter what it is. Just having a Dream, any Dream, is good enough.

But of course this is not what life—or the Bible— teaches us! Any Dream will *not* do. Certain Dreams can destroy people's lives... Think of the horrific consequences of Hitler's Dream of a "pure" German race. Even a Dream from the Dream Giver needs to be handled responsibly. We cannot do simply what we like with our Dreams.

His name was Howard Hughes, and the name of his Dream was *more.* He wanted more money, so he invested his enormous inheritance and increased it in just a few years to a billion dollars. He wanted more fame, so he went to Hollywood and became a filmmaker and a star. He wanted more sensual pleasure, so he used his fabulous wealth to buy women and any form of sensual pleasure he desired. He wanted to experience more excitement, so he designed, built, and piloted the fastest aircraft of his time.

Hughes could dream of anything money could buy— and get it. He firmly believed that *more* would make him happy. But he mistook the pleasure of *more for oneself* for the joy of *bigger than oneself*. His Dream was not significant enough to bring meaning to his life.

In his old age, Hughes became an eccentric recluse, emaciated and unkempt, with decaying teeth and long, twisted fingernails. Countless needle marks all over his body testified to his drug addiction. But until his death he held onto his destructive Dream that more possessions would bring more fulfillment.

Perhaps Joseph also thought at first that he could do what he liked with his Dreams. When we meet him in Genesis, he is the spoiled, tattling apple of his father's eye who insensitively boasts to his elder brothers, "Listen to the Dream I had! I'm going to be more important than you! You are all going to come and bow down to me." From this, his brothers came to the "obvious" conclusion: Not only is he Dad's blue-eyed boy, but God favors him above us, too.

Your Dream can cause harm if you confine it to your little world and your selfish heart—instead of trying to discover what the Dream Giver wants to achieve through you with this Dream.

WHEN IS YOUR DREAM BIG ENOUGH?

Almost all parents have Dreams for their children. You might picture your son standing on a podium with a gold medal around his neck or your daughter playing the piano, enthralling an audience. You might have a vision of your child having some kind of important job, with the security of a good salary, medical insurance, and a retirement fund. You might hope that your child will one day find love and enjoy a happy family life.

There is only one thing wrong with such Dreams: They are not big enough to *inspire* a child. Perhaps these Dreams leave your children stone cold or excite them only for a little while. *Only Dreams that give real meaning to their lives and those of others are "big enough" to be true Life Dreams.*

This also holds true for the Dreams your children dream for themselves: that sports car or that moment when the whole world worships them as "idols". . . If they dream such Dreams and fail to realize them, young people run the risk of becoming bitter. And even if they do come true, they are so shallow that your child will be dogged by a sense of emptiness and meaninglessness.

The ever-present danger of a Dream going in the wrong direction is rooted not so much in the Dream itself as in the way we understand and live our Dreams. For example, a child dreaming of becoming a doctor could be seeing it as a Dream about status and lifestyle. I call this a Small Dream: a dream concerning only oneself and one's personal desires. Even if this Dream is realized, it will not bring true satisfaction. But what if this child came to *understand* the same Dream differently—as a Dream of healing, of reaching out to people and making a difference in a broken world? Then it becomes a part of the Dream Giver's Big Dream for the whole of creation.

Recently, I read about a nine-year-old boy who with

his family pursued a Dream that brought special meaning to his young life—and the lives of countless other children.

Mackenzie Snyder grew up in a family where love and kindness were the norm. He was only in second grade when his parents encouraged him and his two brothers to enter an international writing competition on the topic "I dream of making the world a better place to live." They reached the finals and went with their parents to Paris to represent the United States at a world conference for children. There Mackenzie met two children who lived in a children's home. They shared with him what it was like to be taken away from home to a place of safety because your parents were unable to take care of you.

When the social workers came to get you, the two children told him, not only were you separated from your parents and siblings, but you also lost your friends and most of the toys and clothes you were used to. What touched Mackenzie's heart was the fact that the children were given only a black garbage bag to pack the few belongings they were allowed to take with them. They used a black trash bag, too, when they were placed with foster families for the holidays.

Mackenzie's parents were as upset as he was when they heard this. "Garbage bags are meant for garbage, not for children to use as travel bags. This could make the children lose their self-respect," his father said. Right then and there Mackenzie discovered a Dream in his heart that the Dream Giver had placed there—and his parents encouraged him to make it come true.

Back in the States, with his mother's help, Mackenzie began searching for secondhand backpacks at garage sales. Whenever he explained that he wanted to send them to welfare organizations that placed children in foster homes and children's homes, people usually let him have them for free. After a while, Mackenzie realized that children who were being sent to strange places surely would welcome a soft toy to help reassure and comfort them. He started looking out for a "cuddly" to put in every backpack he sent. Every bag also contained a personal note from him. When he was in third grade, he and his family, together with the local welfare, arranged a "Bring a Backpack for a Foster Child" Day. This caught the attention of the press...and Mackenzie's Dream took off in a big way.

These days, several churches, companies, and schools sponsor Mackenzie. With the help of his parents, brothers, and a large number of volunteers, thousands of backpacks have been sent out. His project is called "Children to Children," and his Big Dream is to send a backpack to every one of the 530,000 youngsters in the United States who are in foster care.[2]

Little Mackenzie has sprinkled the gold dust of his Dream into the far corners of the land. At the age of nine he is a joyful and fulfilled, focused child.

Many people lead frustrating, empty lives because they are trying to confine a Big Dream within the limits of their own selfishness, turning it into a Small

Dream. If you as parent are satisfied with your children's Small Dreams, you are conditioning them to eventually not expect anything much of themselves—or of life itself.

Flea trainers exploit this same truth by placing a flea in a screw top bottle. Initially the flea will jump as high as possible trying to get out, hitting the lid every time. Quickly, though, the flea becomes conditioned to restrict the height of its jumps to just below the lid so as not to injure itself. As soon as this happens, if the trainer removes the lid, the flea will stay in the bottle. The reflex to jump is still there, but the flea will never jump high enough to escape. Even though the lid is no longer there, the flea *believes* it is...

Do you want your child to be satisfied with a Small Dream?

THE DREAM GIVER'S DREAM

Joseph's early Dreams were in fact nothing more than clues. They got Joseph to start picturing himself as a leader, but revealed nothing of the *purpose* of his leadership. Joseph came to understand this purpose only when, after considerable hardship, his Dream had been fulfilled. Only then did he perceive that "it was to save lives that God sent me ahead of you" (Genesis 45:5, NIV). It never was a case of God favoring him above his brothers. No, God wanted to demonstrate his love for them all *through* Joseph. God's Dream was to conquer famine, thus saving people from extinction and introducing them to Joseph's loving God.

Your Dream is like a piece of a jigsaw puzzle the Dream Giver is building. Looking at your piece in isolation, it often doesn't make sense. Only by seeing the full picture and how your piece fits into it will you understand what your piece is all about. Similarly, as a parent you have to see that the Dream Giver dreams about healing humankind and healing Creation before you will be able to determine how your Dreams and your children's Dreams fit into the whole.

Often the Dream Giver's way of working restoration is to use the seemingly inconspicuous, unimportant things that the world ignores or sneers at to realize His Dream. It is typical of the Dream Giver to achieve Great Things through Small Acts of obedience by ordinary people in whose hearts he has placed a Big Dream.

I know of a man who made a huge impact in his workplace by living out God's commandment to be charitable. Justice La Guardia was from New York. An anecdote about him tells about the day a poverty-stricken man appeared before him on a charge of stealing two loaves of bread and some processed meat from a supermarket. His defense was that he was out of work and had no food to feed his family. He had tried but couldn't find help anywhere.

"Well, I have no choice but to sentence you," said Judge La Guardia. "You have broken the law, which allows for no exceptions. I therefore have to fine you twenty dollars." The man's eyes widened with shock. He had no money, and the only alternative was a jail sentence. Then Judge La Guardia put his hand in his pocket and added, "And here is the money to pay the fine. Further, I fine everyone in this court two dollars because they live in a city where men without work have to steal to eat."

He placed another twenty dollars in his empty drinking glass and gave it to the court orderly to pass around the court. The man left with a bundle of bills in his hand and the light of heaven shining in his eyes.[3]

COMFORT ZONES ARE DANGEROUS

In my book *The Dream Giver,* I make the point that if we always want to remain comfortable, we'll never be able to really live our Dreams. Therefore, teach your children to cross the Borders of their Comfort Zones when their Dreams demand it—which often involves having to break through a Wall of Fear.

Remember where Joseph's Dream began to go wrong? His father and brothers (and apparently he was equally guilty) never actually tried to find out what the Dream Giver's purpose was for Joseph's Dreams—these indications of Joseph's future as a leader. His brothers felt threatened in their Comfort Zones by their younger brother's Dreams. The familiar way of doing things was that elder brothers were in charge and younger brothers remained underlings. That was what Joseph's brothers were comfortable with.

Even Jacob became upset when his favorite son challenged his position of authority as head of the family. Joseph's second Dream shook Jacob's Comfort Zone, too. Even after he had rebuked Joseph, Jacob and his other sons remained uneasy: "His brothers were jealous of him, but his father kept the matter in mind" (Genesis 37:10–11, NIV). But the brothers' thoughts turned into action. They reacted aggressively because they felt threatened. Later, when they met Joseph on his own in the fields, they said, "'Here comes that dreamer!. . . Come now, let's kill him and throw him into one of these cisterns. . . . Then we'll see what comes of his dreams'" (vv. 19–20, NIV).

We feel at home in our Comfort Zones, but living a Big Dream demands that we set out for the unfamiliar. This makes us feel unsure and unsafe—and no one likes that. So we abandon our Dream Journey and return to what we find familiar and comfortable. But every time we do this, it becomes more difficult to leave the Comfort Zone and live the Dream. That's when we start limiting our children and ourselves to Small Dreams, which cannot give real meaning to life.

The Danish philosopher Søren Kierkegaard strikingly illustrates the danger of Comfort Zones in his parable of the tame and wild geese.

One year, in spring, a wild goose flew with its flock northward across Europe. On their long flight, the flock descended to the Danish plains to take a small rest beside a barn where a number of tame geese were living. This wild goose particularly enjoyed the comfort of an abundance of juicy corn and the protection of the barn against the strong wind. When its friends took off again, it decided to stay for just another hour or so. The hour became a day, a week, a month...eventually the good food and the safe barn made the goose decide to remain for the whole summer.

In the autumn, the flock of wild geese winged past again on their journey south. When the goose on the ground heard their cries, almost forgotten feelings of joy and excitement gripped it. With much flapping of wings, the wild goose took off to join its friends in free flight. But the corn had made it fat—it could reach no higher than the barn's roof. So the goose landed with a bump on the ground, consoling itself: "Flying may be wonderful, and life on the ground may be pretty boring, but it is safe here and the food is good."

Every spring and autumn after that, when it heard the honking of the wild geese in flight, its eyes began to blink and its wings involuntarily began to flap. Dimly, as in a long-forgotten dream, it once again remembered how wonderful it felt swooping so high in the sky...

Eventually the day dawned when it heard the call of the wild geese without paying the slightest attention. When winter came that year, the cook arrived in search of a fat goose, and the tame wild goose ended up as a tasty Christmas meal on the farmer's table.[4]

Don't let your children become tamed wild geese in their Comfort Zones. They were made to fly!

BREAKING THROUGH THE WALL OF FEAR

When you first hold your child in your arms, experiencing an overwhelming desire to protect this tiny, defenseless baby from the world is perfectly fine and is how it should be. The problem is that in some parents' minds, their children never progress beyond the diaper stage. They overprotect them, trying to make them always feel safe. They create Comfort Zones for their children, communicating this message: "You stay here in your nice Comfort Zone. Mom and Dad will take care of all the risk-taking in the big world out there." More often than not, the Wall of Fear hemming our children in is our own handiwork.

Often we are the ones who handed our children the scissors of selfishness they use to trim down their Dreams into Small Dreams. "I just want the best for my child" is many parents' motto. But are safety, comfort, and Small Dreams really "the best" for them? What, then, should a parent do? Here are a few basics:

- *When you dream with your children, always keep the Dream Giver's Big Dream in mind.* Talk to them about how their Dreams fit in with God's.
- *Know your children's Comfort Zones and Walls of Fear.* Don't push them towards their Borders just for the fun of it—be there when they need help to break out of their Comfort Zones and through their Walls of Fear. Encourage them and praise every effort they make to break out on their own.

✤ *Break free of the notion that you must fulfill all your children's needs or that you have to protect them from every difficulty.* In order to become unselfish adults, children must learn that there are other people in the world, too, and that there is more to life than their own needs. Avoid being the kind of parents who treat their grown sons and daughters as if they were babies—all they have to do is yell and they'll get exactly what they want. Take a good look at your parenting style. You could be smothering your child in a cozy Comfort Zone.

✤ *Set your children free from the need for false security by offering the genuine security of your love.* For children to be able to face a Wall of Fear they must know that you understand and accept them and that you care. Children often are afraid to take a chance because they are unsure of themselves, not having the assurance of their parents' unconditional love.

✤ *Create an oasis for your children where they can renew their strength.* Youngsters struggling to break out of their Comfort Zones often become worn out and downhearted. Be sensitive to this; provide for times of rest when you can inspire each other to carry on dreaming.

SECRET NUMBER 3: EXPLORE

EXPLORE all the life-areas your children are good at or that excite them—clear indicators of the made-to-fit Dreams that God put in their hearts.

People who apparently are "lucky" enough to have attained great success often will tell you it had little to do with "luck." It much rather was a case of them having had a natural interest in a particular direction; out of this a dream began to take shape and they began to work passionately and enthusiastically at realizing that dream. The only "luck" involved was that they knew someone who had faith in their vision.
ALAN LLOYD McGINNIS

❧

Queen Victoria said of British Prime Minister William Gladstone,
"When I was with him, I felt as if I was in the
company of one of the greatest leaders in the world."
On Premier Benjamin Disraeli, however, she remarked,
"When I was with him, he made me feel as if I was one
of the greatest leaders in the world.
Consequently, his term of office was the
best time of my entire reign."

She was born with Down's syndrome. You realize this the moment you meet her. But it doesn't seem to bother her at all. She is a cheerful person, riding all over town on her bicycle running errands for her mother. She earns her own spending money delivering newspapers. At church she is an active member of the Bible study group, and she teaches the preschool group at Sunday school.

When asked how she managed to raise such a positive child, her mother replies, "I concentrate on what she can do rather than fret over the things she can't do. I have always tried to remember that she, too, is a talented person, someone with God-given gifts that can be developed."

Every child has at least some talent and interests. They offer important clues for parents trying to establish what Dream the Dream Giver has woven into their child's being. Your task is to teach your children to regard their unique gifts as tools for discovering and fulfilling their Dreams.

"EVERYTHING HE (JOSEPH) DID..."

Joseph's brothers decided to get rid of "that dreamer" (see story in Genesis 37–47). Consequently, Joseph landed in a well, then became a slave in Egypt, and finally ended up in jail—not a pleasant path to take and enough to make *anyone* lose faith in Dreams. But time and time again Joseph came out on top. Having been sold as a slave, he was then put in charge of the entire household of the captain of Pharaoh's guard. Having been thrown into jail for no better reason than being loyal to his master, he was then put in charge of all the prisoners. Jacob was clearly right to regard Joseph as a born leader. No matter where he ended up, he became a leader.

In Genesis 39:2 we find the most important reason for Joseph's success: "The LORD was with Joseph." The Dream Giver never once abandoned Joseph to his fate, not in the well or when he became a slave, not even in prison.

But there is a second reason for Joseph's success, and it flows from the first: Twice we read of everything Joseph *did* (Genesis 39:3, 23). Joseph was not a mere Dreamer; he used his talents and worked to succeed, even though he often found himself in the most adverse circumstances. He actively pursued his Dream.

Alan Lloyd McGinnis, writer of a number of

successful motivational books, says, "We have no control over the hand life deals us—but using our mind and our willpower and our faith, we can determine *how* we play even the worst cards."

God's presence in our lives does not allow us to sit back and watch Him do it all. God sets us to work because He wants us to develop the gifts He gave us to their fullest potential.

I believe that God wants parents to play a similar role in their children's lives. We shouldn't try to do everything for our children. Rather, we should allow them the freedom to discover what they can do themselves and to develop the self-confidence to *actively* pursue their Dreams.

AN IMPORTANT WARNING

It might be a good thing for all parents to be issued a written warning at every child's birth: *Handle with care this precious child by respecting his or her unique gifts as well as limitations.* Parents all too often become so frustrated with their children's limitations that they forget all about their gifts. Such an attitude makes a child think, *To earn my father and mother's approval, I can't be myself.* If you keep putting across this message—even without actually saying it—*I wish you were different. I wish you were more like...*, you are actually standing in the way of your children discovering their Dreams.

As we have seen, Jacob was right on target when he

gave Joseph his Dreamcoat. Because he loved his son so well, he could discern his natural talent for leadership. In this way he made Joseph aware of his special gift, too.

Perhaps Jacob did this because he knew from bitter experience how awful it was to have your parents wish you were different. As a young boy, Jacob had to pass himself off as his brother, Esau, to receive his father, Isaac's, blessing. He had to dress up as Esau, smell like Esau, and even make his arms as hairy—otherwise his father would never have blessed him (see Genesis 27).

It was only years later, when Jacob wrestled with God at the ford of the Jabbok, that he received a blessing in his own right. The Dream Giver blesses you and every one of your children individually, exactly as you are. But parents so often repeat Isaac's mistake. They require their children to live up to parental expectations before they will accept them as "good enough."

Unfortunately, Jacob learned only half his lesson. He most certainly blessed Joseph with the Dreamcoat for being himself, but he neglected doing the same for his other children.

Every now and then I meet people who feel frustrated because they know they are in the wrong line of work. They confess, "I really wanted to be a teacher, but my father says teachers earn too little. On top of it, he wanted me to follow in his footsteps. I had to become an attorney..." Or, "All I've ever wanted to do is arrange flowers, but Dad said, 'Over my dead body; that is no job for a man!'"

I am reminded of the film *Billy Elliot* (rated R for language). This eleven-year-old son of a poor widower from a small English mining town had an "otherwise" Dream. His father and elder brother were participating in a strike for a living wage, but they scrimped and saved so that Billy could have boxing lessons because they believed that was "the thing for boys." One afternoon, on his way to the boxing club, Billy walked past a room in the same building where a ballet class was in progress. To his own surprise, a Dream he had been completely unaware of sprang to life in him.

Something about the movement and the music captivated him. With her keen eye for talent, the ballet teacher noticed that the boy who came every day to watch was spontaneously moving gracefully to the music. She persuaded Billy to exchange his boxing gloves for ballet shoes. In the meantime, his father and brother lost all income because of their participation in the strike. When they found out that their hard earned savings were no longer being used for boxing, but for a girly thing like ballet, they exploded in anger, derided Billy, and forbade him to carry on dancing.

In sheer frustration at his family's complete failure to understand his Dream, Billy found his release in a brilliant dance sequence on the roof of a nearby building. Fortuitously, his father saw him and was overcome by guilt, realizing that he had misjudged his son's unmistakable talent and held him up to ridicule. Fortunately it was not too late to put things right, and with the unexpected support of his mining buddies, Billy's father found the money to take his son to an audition at a London ballet school. . .

Fifteen years later, Billy's father and his tough-guy brother sat in the audience as the curtain opened on a ballet performance in London's West End—with Billy in the leading role.

Do not thoughtlessly put down your children's unique *talents.* Respect their *limitations,* too, for only God has no limitations. Rather, help them discover their particular gifts and interests, even if these are completely different from what you would have preferred. For the Dream Giver created them for a Dream—a Dream that you did not design, but that you can explore with them.

Parental love implies the ability to celebrate your child's individuality.

DISCOVERING GIFTS

Parents can help their children discover their gifts in two ways. One way is to push them: "Son, you can't pass up this opportunity!"; "My girl, I am sure you will just love doing that!" This approach can cause fundamental problems. Children may fake excitement simply to please their parents. But they will lose interest as soon as the parents stop pushing them, because their motivation was external—it did not arise from any natural talent or interest.

A better way to help your children is to *discover with*

them—and *with the Dream Giver*—the direction their gifts point them. The words "The LORD was with Joseph" remind us that the Dream Giver is always by our side, offering help and opportunities for success, allowing for failure. And in the process, every Dreamer's gifts become evident, and we realize for ourselves where our interests lie. Try being such a Dream Builder for your children. Guide them on their journey of discovering their gifts and interests, and they will find their own motivation to try things out—and succeed.

Parents can do a number of things to assist their children in this thrilling quest:

Play with them from early childhood, but allow them to take the lead in the game. When you observe your kids' play patterns, you will soon see what excites them and what bores them. Also, look through books with them to see what holds their attention and what leaves them cold. In this way you can discover, even when they still are tiny, something about your children's natural inclinations.

Cultivate an interest in the things that fascinate your children. As your children grow older, you will see what their real interests are. Some pursuits turn out to be one-day wonders. For example, they buy a guitar, but in a month it lies gathering dust in a corner. Other interests last longer, falling into a permanent pattern. Encourage your children in these by letting their excitement rub off on you. In this way you might help shape a vague Dream into Something Big.

Allow your children the freedom to express their strong points.
Every child needs to experience success. When children
enjoy some small victories—even in areas that seem
minor to you—your praise and encouragement will boost
their self-confidence, which may overflow into other
areas of their lives. But if you continually bombard your
children with criticism about their weak points, they will
experience a sense of failure that may eventually destroy
their talents and interests as well. Well-known writer and
child psychologist Dr. James Dobson feels very strongly
about parents' responsibility to encourage their children
to try excelling in at least one area.

Dobson tells that in primary school he was a sickly
little guy with matchstick-thin arms and legs and was "so
shy that I wanted to die if anyone so much as looked at
me." But one day his father saw him hitting a tennis ball
with reasonable accuracy against the wall in their
backyard. He started taking James every Saturday to the
tennis courts, where he spent hours with him making him
hit hundreds of balls over the net. "I'm extremely grateful
to my father," Dobson wrote in one of his *Focus on the
Family* books, "for noticing some talent in me—and for
keeping me practicing. From then on there was one thing
that made me feel good about myself: I might have been
skinny and shy, but I was the best tennis player in sixth
grade."[5]

If children are not strong academically, parents can
help them discover a lifelong interest or aptitude in

another field, like music or another art form, a sport, or some type of community service.

Help your children to see the connection between their talents and interests and their Dreams. You can say things like, "It seems to me the other children feel comfortable telling you their problems. Would you perhaps like to be a psychologist?" Or, "I've noticed that you really enjoy books about animals. Have you ever thought of becoming a vet one day?"

Director Steven Spielberg (*ET, Jurassic Park, Schindler's List*) was hopeless at sports, and his peer group often teased him. His mother had noticed an early fascination with photography and that the boy was blessed with a powerful imagination. She believed that an undiscovered but very special Dream was hidden somewhere inside him. So she bought Steven a small camera and encouraged him to take not just random photos, but to weave stories around the pictures. It quickly became evident that young Steven had a natural aptitude in this direction, and his mother built up the concealed Dream by making a big fuss of his efforts. "We used to wander around in the desert for days so he could take photos, endless photos," she recounts. "It was fun for both of us, and he thrived on it.

"Then one day we bought him a movie camera..."

Children who are taught that even the "smallest" gifts didn't just fall into their laps but are part of a much bigger picture quickly learn to see themselves as people of ability who are capable of succeeding at what they undertake.

COUNT YOUR WORDS!

"Count your words, because every word you say counts." I read these unforgettable words in Peter J. Daniels's well-known book *Mrs. Phillips, You Were Wrong!* Peter's seventh grade teacher, Mrs. Phillips, kept telling him, "You are the rotten apple in the basket. Your stupidity is corrupting the whole class. You'll never amount to anything." Peter believed her and dropped out of school, without learning to read and write properly.

And his life indeed could have turned out a complete failure if it weren't for his father, who refused to give up on him. Over the years he restored his son's self-esteem through dedicated attention and words of encouragement, creating opportunities for Peter to feel that he, too, was able to do something right. His father's positive attitude eventually cancelled out the harm the teacher had done, and Peter ultimately became a successful businessman. Yet he never forgot Mrs. Phillips's hurtful words, as is evident from the title of his bestseller.

Our words—often the words we say without thinking—can make or break our children. With just a few words, you can reinforce your children's image of themselves as gifted people fully equipped to live out their Dreams—or you can break their spirit. In *Teenage Boys,* Bill Beausay offers the following list of "Dream Breakers" and "Dream Builders." Which list resembles the way you talk to your children?

DREAM BREAKERS	DREAM BUILDERS
Why?	Why not?
It won't work out.	It could work!
That's not how we do things.	We can start doing things differently.
It's impossible.	It could be possible!
That's stupid.	Wow, that sounds really interesting.
You're just a Dreamer...	You're a genius!
That is so unrealistic.	I just love your Big Dreams!
What utter nonsense!	I don't really understand?
That is a really dumb idea.	What a wonderful idea!
It will take you forever.	When can we start working on it?
It's too far.	It's closer than you think.
We don't have that kind of money.	Perhaps we can find you a sponsor.
Life has destroyed my Dreams.	I'm taking my life back and I want to help you keep your Dreams alive.

MORE THAN WORDS

But encouragement isn't just words. Lots of hugs and finding that extra time to enjoy something with your child can work wonders. It's important for your children to know that you don't expect superhuman feats from them. When you say you believe that hidden somewhere inside them is a Dream just waiting to be awakened, they need to understand that you are talking about their natural talents and interests, which you just want them to express to the full. The message you want to communicate isn't, "You *must* become this or that!" It's something like, "Just be exactly *who you are*   for in your uniqueness lies the precious Dream that the Dream Giver has placed in your heart."

CELEBRATE YOUR CHILDREN

We live in an era that celebrates celebrities. Ordinary children can easily be made to feel drab and colorless compared to the glamorous creatures filling magazines and TV screens. Therefore, teach your children to think of themselves, with their unique talents and interests, as *natural* "celebrities" by celebrating who they are.

Give a round of applause for the special individuals the Dream Giver has created in your children, for the Dreams He has given them, and for the wonderful way He has equipped them to live their Dreams. Wrap a gorgeous, multicolored Dreamcoat around your children!

SECRET NUMBER 4:
AFFIRM

AFFIRM your own belief in your children's Dreams by exposing them to all the available *information and experiences* that will help them define their Dreams.

The place where God is calling you is that place where your deepest joy meets the deepest need of the world.

FREDERICK BUECHNER

∾

Humility is the strangest thing.
The moment you think you have it, it is gone.

ROY B. ZUCK

∞

I believe that the yardstick of greatness is humility.
By "humility," I do not mean a lack of faith in your abilities or
hesitation in putting forward your point of view. But really great
men and women are aware of their own powerlessness.

They realize fully that the source of their greatness is not located in
them, but rather functions through them; that they cannot be
otherwise, or greater—or smaller—than God has made them.

JOHN RUSKIN

All my life I have swung like a pendulum between all and nothing," she said. "In my parents' home I was all-important. I saw this as my right. Then I started school and found out that I was not the smartest, or the prettiest, or the fastest. I was just another child—and I felt like nothing."

She was quiet for a moment. "It's still the same. When someone pays me a compliment, I feel like I'm queen of the world. But when no one notices me, I feel completely worthless. I just keep shuttling between all and nothing."

A baby is the center—all—of its little world. But at some point, we all have to learn that we are not all that important. We have to learn humility. But then we run the risk of misunderstanding humility, of thinking it means we are nothing. But you aren't a mere nothing; you are somebody special—a unique individual created by the

Dream Giver for a unique Dream.

We must teach our children to walk the middle path between all and nothing. Sometimes they are like hot-air balloons: somewhere up high in the sky and completely out of reach. Sometimes their Dreams are just castles in the sky, bearing no resemblance to real life or their true nature. Then our task is to bring them down to earth, lovingly but firmly.

At other times, they have already fallen flat on their faces and feel like worms—utter nothings. A Dream has failed to come true, and now they don't want to hear a thing about dreaming. In such a situation, parents need to know how to help their children to their feet and reassure them once again: "My child, you are not nothing. You are somebody special. What you achieve outwardly is not as important as who you are inside."

BETWEEN THE DREAM AND THE BOTTOM OF THE WELL

When Joseph received his Dream about becoming a leader, he started acting big. One might be able to imagine him boasting about his special coat and his special Dreams. But before he knew it, Joseph was at the bottom of a well, brought back to earth with a bump—in fact, almost buried alive. All was reduced to nothing. After that, Joseph became a slave in Egypt. A true nobody, as a slave was a mere possession, a number. But perhaps the dark pit of despair helped Joseph realize that even a slave could be somebody. Because despite Joseph being a mere nothing, God blessed whatever he undertook, and he became a figure of authority in his master's house— only to end up in jail for his trouble. Reduced to nothing once more. But even in jail Joseph pursued what he was born to do: lead.

This is also how we and our children learn that we all are somebody—through both the unfortunate experiences that bring us crashing down to earth *and* our successes. We can guide our children through this process in two ways:

Believe in their Dreams. Then we will be able to help them to *interpret* both positive and negative experiences in light of their vision of themselves and their Dreams, as well as to *integrate* these experiences into this vision.

Consciously *expose them to experiences that will help them draw a clearer picture of their Dreams.*

HELP YOUR CHILD UNDERSTAND LIFE

Children have to handle a barrage of good and bad experiences. Often they perceive what they are going through in extreme terms: all or nothing. A good experience might send their hot-air balloon soaring; a bad one might make them feel like they've hit rock bottom. Children that never learn to handle events sensibly simply continue to immaturely seesaw their way through life.

This doesn't mean you have to be a spoilsport when your children encounter the highs of life. If your daughter comes dancing through the door because she has been selected for the first basketball team, you don't have to deliver a sermon on humility. And if after long and taxing exams, your son hears that he has achieved the highest marks in his class, it is not your sacred duty to remind him that worldly fame is of little value. Some parents are grey, wet blankets, dampening their children's joy in life just because they don't want them to become bigheaded.

Yet it also happens that people—including children— experience intense disappointment after having great success. The reason is probably that they expected their achievements to make them feel better about themselves, but they didn't do the trick. Or they wanted the thrill to last and were disappointed at how quickly the excitement faded. At the deepest level, however, the reason for this kind of disappointment is that success in itself lacks meaning.

The tragic life of the English poet Lord Byron (1788–1824) is a classic example of this. His brilliant poetry, together with his personal charisma and flamboyant lifestyle, brought him renown all over Europe. He had free access to money, honor, and every pleasure in life. Shortly before his relatively early death at age thirty-six, he looked back on his "successful" life and wrote:

> Drank every glass of pleasure and excitement to the dregs. Started early and carried on drinking, drinking *all* that life had to offer in the way of wealth and fame. And then, died of thirst.

Nothing I had drunk could quench my thirst.
And there was nothing left to drink.[6]

Help your children discover the meaning *of success the following ways:*

Teach your children what gifted *really means.* Children must come to understand that our talents are really gifts from God that equip us for living our Dreams. Pleasure in any achievement fades quickly. But if your children can relate their happiness to a celebration of the Giver of all gifts, who makes our successes possible, they will discover lasting joy. Joy in God's goodness is not the opposite of pleasure in our achievements; rather, it adds depth to our pleasure and strengthens it.

Help them see how small successes and positive experiences fit in with their Big Dream. Joseph's success in Potiphar's household and in jail undoubtedly prepared him for the moment when his Dream of being a leader would reach fulfillment. If your children could regard each victory, however small, as a little step toward the realization of their Big Dream, they would learn to cherish not just the great successes. If they could realize that every experience helps prepare them for what the Dream Giver has in store, it would all start making so much more sense.

That is why it is so important to expose children to information and experiences that will help define their Dreams. When you have discovered the direction of their Dreams, expose your kids to books, people, films, videos,

productions, TV programs, dramas, music—whatever
suits their field of interest—that will stir up excitement
about their Dream. As the Italian proverb goes:

Only those who feel their Dreams
are equipped to follow them.

*Help your children understand that we are blessed in order to bless
others.* The Dream that the Dream Giver has given you is
designed to meet a Big Need somewhere in the world.
Joseph's Dream of becoming a leader corresponded
exactly with the needs created by the famine that struck
Egypt and Canaan. Your children's Dreams also
correspond to some needs somewhere in the world—and
if they can learn to see their successes in this light, they
will find so much more meaning in success.

A child who performs well academically, for
example, could realize that her intellectual gifts might
make her suitable for a career in medical research or
law—opportunities that could help many people. A
sports star, actor, or comedian could come to see how
much pleasure his achievements bring other people.
Whatever the profession or trade your child wishes to
follow one day, keep them aiming for a more important
goal than earning a good income. Help them shape their
Dreams in such a way that one day, in one way or
another, it can be said of them what the people of
Lambaréné in Gabon said of the great missionary
doctor Albert Schweitzer:

When he first came here, there was no light.
When he left no darkness remained.

There are countless examples of people blessed with good intellect, special abilities, or privileged circumstances who as a token of their gratitude decided to invest in society. Inspire your children with stories like these. For example, a highly skilled and intelligent young surgeon from Cape Town decided to forego his comfortable lifestyle and offer his skills in some of the most primitive field hospitals in the world. The gripping book of his experiences is called *The Dressing Station.* Dr. Jonathan Kaplan's Dream has taken him to the front lines of the war between the Kurds and Saddam Hussein's Republican Guard, and places such as Eritrea, the Amazon, Burma, and Mozambique.

Of course, world-shattering deeds are not the only way to bless others. Remind your children that perfectly ordinary people can do out-of-the-ordinary things to make the world a better place.

In pursuing their Dreams, your children will encounter negative experiences, too. What should you do when they come home telling you they didn't make the team or failed their exams? How can you help them face life again when they feel like nothings? Here are a few simple things to remember:

Embrace your children with your love. Strikingly, the Bible emphasizes God's presence in Joseph's life *particularly during the difficult times* during his service to Potiphar and while in jail—people saw that "the LORD was with him" (Genesis 39:3, 21). At a time when others easily could have treated Joseph as just a number, he remained a precious somebody to his loving God. When your children are feeling low, devoting your love and time to them is the best way to help them rediscover that they are somebody.

Help your children accept their limitations while holding on to their potential. Teach them to accept that they are human beings, not superheroes, and that they will need others for as long as they live. When asked what he ascribed his phenomenal success in business to, millionaire John D. Rockefeller always answered, "To others." Explain to your children that it is perfectly acceptable to make mistakes and to feel afraid or dejected sometimes. It is part of being human to ask others for help or advice or comfort. Children must not be made to feel that they have to do it all under their own steam—neither must they be made to believe that they are capable of nothing.

Help your children learn from disappointment and negative experiences. The message you want to communicate is, "We can't always avoid bad experiences, and we can't change the past. What we can do is learn from our mistakes—and use this as training for realizing our Dreams."

The nineteenth-century Scottish historian and writer Thomas Carlyle spent six years writing his masterpiece on the French Revolution. On completion, he took the bulk of the manuscript to his friend John Stuart Mill and asked for his opinion. A day or so later, while Mill was out, the domestic help found the manuscript lying next to his chair in his study. She gathered up the pile of papers, together with other "rubbish," and threw them into the fire. And that was in the days before computers!

When Mill realized what had happened, he went to break the news to Carlyle in a state of shock. Carlyle listened calmly. Smiling weakly, he said, "Never mind, John, these things happen. I'll start over again. It is all somewhere in my head, no doubt."

When his friend had gone, Carlyle's wife saw him leaning against the window, sighing heavily. Then he said out loud, "Oh well, the manuscript is gone. I had better start again." Straightening his shoulders, he lifted his chin and sat down at his desk. Once again, he took up his pen. . .

Over a very long period, with dogged determination, Carlyle once again completed the series of books on the French Revolution, and the work—titled *The French Revolution*—became one of the great classics of our time.

Carlyle was not only a great writer; he was a great enough man not to let this huge disappointment get the better of him. He put it behind him and carried on living his Dream.

Show your children that you still believe in their Dreams, no matter what has gone wrong. It is often better to *do* something practical to show them that you have not given up than to try *talking* them back into following their Dreams. Remember the mother I mentioned in an earlier chapter, the one who gave her seriously injured son a pair of running shoes instead of a stream of words? Those shoes encouraged that injured athlete to run again. Kids' experience of life is limited, therefore they are prone to perceive any setback as a shot through the heart. But you can help them see past the current setback to the Dreams beckoning them into the future. Remind them often of Robert Ingersoll's famous definition of true courage:

> The decisive test for true courage
> is to lose without losing courage.

Expose Your Children to Experience

A practical way to help shape your children's Dreams is to expose them to experiences that could either bring them down to earth or inspire them. For example, a certain mother had serious misgivings about some aspects of her daughter's Dream. A biography of Florence Nightingale had inspired the girl to such an extent that she insisted on becoming a nurse. After talking with her, her mother realized that this teenager was picturing herself with a lamp in a darkened hospital ward, wiping the foreheads of good-looking men. In her daughter's final year of school, the mother arranged for her to take a casual job at the hospital during the holidays. This experience brought the girl down to earth with a bump; it made her realize that she was not cut out for the drudgery or harsh realities of nursing.

But her mother did not leave the matter there. Together they explored other possibilities until the girl, with her aptitude for science subjects, decided to become a medical researcher—the same Dream, but in a form that suited her better.

In the same way, parents can use positive exposure to help their children get a clearer picture of how their Dream would work out in reality. An animal lover, for example, would be able to make a more informed choice after talking to a veterinary surgeon, taking a holiday job at a zoo, or perhaps spending a short time helping on a farm.

Even more important, this exposure to reality should help children understand the link between their Dreams and God's Big Dream. The Dream Giver puts a Dream into everyone's heart with the intention that eventually this Dream will become a blessing to all.

To this end, it is important that children—especially those from a privileged background—experience firsthand the great need in the world. Children who live protected lives often don't realize how poverty and hunger really could affect a person's life. They also find it very difficult to imagine how their gifts and talents could make a difference in the world.

There is a story of a preacher who went to visit one of the well-off members of his congregation. It was an English winter and bitterly cold outside, but he was well wrapped up in a fur coat. As the visit drew to a close, the preacher told the head of the family that he wished to ask him something confidential. The man accompanied the minister outside without stopping to put on his jacket for what he expected to be a quick good-bye. But the preacher, cozy in his fur coat, began talking about one thing and another until his host was literally shivering with cold. The man repeatedly tried to find out what the preacher wanted to ask him, but the preacher just kept making small talk. "Wouldn't you like to go inside again?" asked the shivering man. But the preacher serenely continued chatting. At last, the head of the household said with chattering teeth, "Reverend, if you don't ask me what you want to right now, I am going to die of cold."

"Sir, I need two hundred dollars to buy a stock of coal for the winter for a family without work."

Immediately the rich man peeled a roll of notes from his wallet and handed it to the preacher with these words, "Reverend, now I know why you left me standing so long out here in the cold. You knew that never in my comfortable life had I been really cold. Now that I have experienced this misery for myself, my heart has opened up to a need I had no notion of earlier..."

You don't have to leave your children standing out in the snow or throw them down a well, but do remember this reality check: *A child that grows up ignorant of the pits of this world won't care about them.*

SECRET NUMBER 5:
MAKE USE

MAKE USE of every opportunity to
help your children learn from *role models*—
positive *and* negative ones.

*She taught me that life can be difficult
and often unfair, but that it still is good to be alive.*

A SON, ABOUT HIS MOTHER

∾

*So, you want to know the secret of successful parenting?
The answer is the same for parents, teachers,
anyone in a leadership position:
Be what you want those who look up to you to be.*

THOMAS CARLYLE

∾

There is no greater influence on the life of a child than a living
example of moral strength. For children to learn to take morality
seriously, they need to see adults living moral lives.

WILLIAM J. BENNETT

*I*t was the evening after their mother's funeral. The
children were grieving, but the atmosphere was neither
grim nor subdued. "Do you remember. . . ?" one said, and
the memories began to flow. There was the time just after
their father had left them and their mother called a family
conference, informing them that they would carry on
come what may. Then there were the times when they
had no food in the house but their mother managed to
put something on the table—and made them laugh over
her strange "emergency cuisine."

"Mom gave me something," the youngest boy said
later, "that I want to hold on to forever. She taught me
that life can be difficult and often unfair, but that it still is
good to be alive."

The wonderful film *Life Is Beautiful* (1998) is the story
of an Italian Jew, Guido Orefice. During the last months
of World War II, he and his young son are taken away by
the Nazis to a concentration camp. With his optimistic
nature, Guido decides to try to protect his child from the
desperate circumstances that lay ahead of them in the

only way he can. He presents to little Giosué a bright world in spite of the horror all around them.

In the truck en route to the camp, Guido tells his son that the trip actually is a surprise for his birthday. They're going on an adventure with an unbelievable prize to be won: a tank—a real, life-size tank! The rules would keep changing, warns Guido, but mostly they will involve hide-and-seek, make-believe, and a special rule called "dead quiet." The people in uniforms they would meet were not really evil, he explained, it was all just part of the game. Sometimes they would be very hungry, too, but this really was a test of endurance for the adventure. Anyone who complained would be disqualified and "sent home."

In this way, Guido managed to keep his little boy's spirits up through the terrors of death, hunger, backbreaking labor, and the inhuman conditions in the barracks. He did everything he could to draw the child's attention to any little "beautiful" incident that could make life bearable. And it worked for him, too. Guido clung to the "realistic" hope that the Allied Forces would come rescue them soon. He succeeded so well in keeping up this life-preserving fantasy for his son that little Giosué believed he had won the "competition" when the first tank of the advancing Allied Forces rolled into the camp and chased away the "make-believe baddies in uniform." The tank driver saw Guido die in the shooting that followed, but lifted the still unsuspecting little boy into the tank with him, letting him sit behind the steering wheel. . .

Of course, all of this is too good to be true. But the film does drive home the point that, through example and influence, parents can teach their children to believe in the beauty of life—no matter how adverse and unfair it sometimes is.

It is a simple but important truth that children learn from what they experience. That is why role models are so decisive in any child's life—and as a parent, you are your child's first role model, for good or evil.

FOLLOW MY EXAMPLE...

As we saw in chapter 3, the Bible tells the story of Joseph for two reasons. The *first and most important* is that it should make us reflect on the words "The LORD was with Joseph" (Genesis 39:2–3, 21, 23). We need to understand clearly that Joseph's Dream was part of God's Big Dream. We learn that God—even when He appeared to have faded into the background—was directing Joseph's life toward the fulfillment of his Dream. The Dream Giver accomplished His purpose with Joseph even though it often seemed as if the Dream of "that dreamer" had been shattered irreparably.

The *second* reason undoubtedly is that we should find inspiration in the words "the LORD gave him success in everything he did" (Genesis 39:3, NIV). Joseph is meant to be an example for us. This doesn't mean he was the image of perfection. Not at all. We are not expected to be "like Joseph" in every respect. But we should note the difference it makes to anybody's life—even if they are reduced to slavery or imprisonment—when God is with them to encourage them to undergo whatever is necessary to realize their Dreams.

From Joseph we learn that what we need in order to live our Dreams is not in the first instance our talents, opportunity, or success upon success. It is simply to believe that God is in our lives and to obey—doing what we were made to do, regardless of our circumstances.

We often think that the way to teach people something is to let them attend a class and then hope that they will apply what they have learned. There is no denying that such classes may be very valuable, but the unfortunate fact is that many people attend one class after another—becoming excited about each one—*without the slightest evidence of change in their lives.*

We learn our most important lessons in the school of life—through the *example* of the *role models* we come in contact with. The Bible is very clear about the value of role models. No disciple could ever forget the evening Jesus spoke to them about being servants. . .and how He practiced what He preached by washing their feet Himself. If you want to teach your children the heart of servanthood, don't preach to them about serving others. Let them see *you* be a servant to others, and you will be telling them, "Follow my example. As I am doing you can do, too. . ."

A young priest wanted St. Francis of Assisi to teach him how to preach. He asked to accompany St. Francis on a preaching visit to a neighboring city to learn by watching him. St. Francis agreed. All day long they walked the streets of the city, chatting and answering questions, visiting homes where there was a need or illness, sometimes offering advice or assistance and on other occasions comfort.

As evening fell, St. Francis said they had to make a start on the return journey. "But the whole day you haven't preached once to anyone or even spoken about Jesus!" the disappointed young priest complained. "I thought you said I was to accompany you to learn to preach!"

"And I hope you did, Brother," replied St. Francis quietly. "If people cannot see our message of Jesus' love in what we do, they will not believe it when we tell them about it. Preaching is of no use if our whole lives aren't sermons."

Your children will discover from the way you live whether you trust the Dream Giver or whether you live as if dreaming makes no sense because Dreams never come true anyway. If you are pessimistic or anxious or just plain disinterested; if you allow the smallest setbacks to get you down; if you distrust other people in principle, your child will follow your example only too easily. Of course, the opposite is true, too. If you live as if you're *passionate* about a Dream you received from the Dream Giver, if you strive to live these Dreams, this attitude will speak far louder to them than words.

A classic German poem subtly illustrates these differing outlooks on life. It goes something like this:

> Two persons had gone on a nature walk. On their return, people wanted to know: "What did you see? Tell us!"
>
> One replied, "Oh, you know, same old mountains and trees, the sun, streams, green grass, blue skies..."
>
> And the other one, "Oh! The mountains and trees! The sun! Streams! Green grass and blue skies!"

A GOOD ROLE MODEL DEFINED

Let me begin by saying what a good role model *isn't. He or she need not be a perfect person who can do absolutely anything.* Only God is perfect and almighty.

Parents who attempt to set a perfect example are actually trying to play God to their children—and we already have seen how catastrophic that is. To be a good role model, you should:

- Be honest about your weaknesses and limitations.
- Openly acknowledge that you are dependent upon God.
- Be prepared to admit that you need other people.

Parents like this will not succumb to cynicism about the world and human fallibility. They will not confuse dependence on God with a passive attitude toward life. And they will not let their need for others degenerate into overdependence—and bitterness when people let them down. Such parents know and also teach their children that:

- God is good. And life, being a gift from God, is good. Indeed, "Life is beautiful."
- Even though you are a weak human being with limitations, you are also a person of talent, designed by the Dream Giver with a unique Dream to live.
- You will disappoint yourself and others often, but God will forgive you each time and bless you with a new beginning for your Dream Journey.
- Other people are sure to disappoint you, but because God has forgiven you, you in turn can forgive them—and embark on a Dream Journey together with them.

This final point highlights one of the most important aspects of being a role model to our children: We must demonstrate through our behavior the lifestyle of people who are able to *receive and offer forgiveness*. If Joseph hadn't forgiven his brothers, his heart would have remained in the well, even when he was occupying a throne in Egypt. People who are unable to receive and offer forgiveness are incapable of realizing their Dreams, too. Even worse, they may realize them partly, but fall short of their true purpose—becoming part of the Dream Giver's Big Dream—because of their bitterness.

Therefore, the most significant role you can play in your children's lives in this respect is to forgive them when they have done wrong, as well as to ask for their forgiveness when you have made a mistake. Parents who consider it beneath them to say, "Sorry, I was wrong," or who are unforgiving toward others, cannot function as positive role models for their children.

A friend tells of a time when his marriage was under great stress. One night he felt he just couldn't take anymore. "I hate you!" he yelled at his wife, completely out of control. "Now you have gone too far. I will never forgive you. Never, ever!"

One day, months later, when peace had been restored between him and his wife, he listened with dismay as his four-year-old son snapped at a friend, "I hate you! Now you have gone too far. I will never forgive you. Never, ever!"

The child was using exactly the same tone of voice he had heard from his bedroom on the night his father had shouted at his mother.

OTHER ROLE MODELS

Being merely human, a parent should not try to be the only role model his or her children need. Their Dreams are unique and therefore different to those of their parents—which means they will need other people as role models as well. The danger here is that our children could inadvertently take the popular route and choose as role models the sensational celebrities from the world of sports or entertainment. These stars often lead superficial lives of luxury and indulge in all sorts of extravagances and provocative antics.

On pages 109–110, I discuss the fact that children, in the process of growing up, come to live in their own worlds more and more and that parents must respect these boundaries. However, children can become too wrapped up in the life they share with their peer group, cutting off any connection to the lives of their parents and other adults. Then they tend to choose their role models exclusively from the youth culture, which may well promote "values" other than those that would help them develop into well-balanced adults of integrity.

The tragedy is that children in the poorest communities—which are often HIV/AIDS-ridden as well—tend to grow up without positive role models. Their parents might have died or be working elsewhere. In these areas it is often the thugs who command respect through violence and seem successful in the materialistic values of our world, having more money than people doing an honest day's work. So they become attractive role models for these children.

This presents parents with some challenges:

Make sure the boundaries between your world and your children's world remain open. Do not let them socialize only with their own age group. Help them get to know other adults, including elderly people. The better children communicate across the generation gap, the greater the chance they will appreciate the value of role models from other generations.

During the apartheid years in South Africa, one day a little black boy was walking down the street with his mother when an elderly white man passed them, smiling and lifting his hat in greeting.

The youngster was astounded: a white man lifting his hat to a black woman and child! "Why did he do that?" he asked his mother.

"It's because he's a priest," she answered.

"Then I also want to be a priest one day," declared the little boy.

The white man was Trevor Huddlestone, then a priest in the black township of Sophiatown, the Harlem of Johannesburg, and a tireless opponent of apartheid. The little black boy was Desmond Tutu.[7]

Expose your child to role models who have been successful in the direction your child's Dream is pointing. Once children have become aware of their own Dreams, adults living similar Dreams in a meaningful way will probably inspire them. For example, if your child has a heart for the poor, introduce him or her to someone who is actively involved in community development.

Encourage your child to read stories (also biographies) or watch films about people who realized their Dreams despite limitations and setbacks. Stimulate their imagination and feed their idealism with tales of people like Agnes Bojaxhiu of Albania. She never attended college, never married, never owned a car. But none of this was necessary for her Dream of helping the poor. She lived her Dream by devoting most of her life to comforting and caring for the poorest of the poor, those dying on the streets. We know her as Mother Teresa of Calcutta, Nobel Prize winner for peace. Today her Dream still inspires thousands.

If there is one book besides the Bible that every family should read and apply, it is William J. Bennett's *The Book of Virtues*. It contains numerous examples of what people living meaningful Dreams have done and said.

Point out to your children those people who have succeeded in making the connection between their own Dreams and the Big Needs of our world. In our society, the rich and glamorous are often held up as examples of people living Dream Lives. This means that squatter camps, AIDS sufferers, and other dark realities of life might seem to our children to be circumstances where no Dream has any chance of coming true. Many turn a blind eye to these harsh realities, holding on to more glittering Dreams. They pursue a selfish Dream that actually serves to help them *get away* from the Big Needs of our world.

Yet, some do take the opposite road. Like Everyman in *The Dream Giver,* they succeed in living their Dreams in the gloomy city of the Anybodies. Your children should know about these people and how satisfying living like that can be! I met a highly qualified woman who teaches by choice in a township school in South Africa. When asked why she didn't use her skills to get a position at a prominent city school, working for a higher salary and in better conditions, she replied, "I love the township kids. They are straightforward; they need my acceptance, love, and attention so much more than children coming from homes where they already have all of that. And they are prepared to work when someone motivates them by helping them discover something to live for. Seeing the Dreams beginning to take shape in their eyes makes it all worth my while."

The important thing to remember about role models for your children is that you can introduce them to suitable people, but you cannot coerce them into becoming inspired by your choices! However, the broader the spectrum of possibilities you introduce them to, the greater the chance that they will find someone who captures their imagination and about whom they can say, "Here is an example I would like to follow."

If you can bring your children to understand that though we are all ordinary people with limitations, the Dream Giver uses each of us in a unique way, you will have given them an inheritance that no one can take away.

Secret Number 6:
Encourage

ENCOURAGE your children to rely on the
Dream Giver as the only Guide who will
show them how to shape their Dreams
to fit in with God's Big Dream for the world.

What is important is not so much what people praise us for,
but what price we are willing to pay for the sake of God.

HENRY WARD BEECHER

❧

I attribute my success mainly to the fact that I was fortunate
enough to realize early in my life that I was not God.

OLIVER WENDELL HOLMES

∾

If you want to give your children the very best heaven and earth
have to offer, surrender them to God's will for their lives.
WILLIAM CAREY

∾

God's will for your children never could lead them anywhere
that his grace could not carry them, too.
ALBERT M. WELLS

ather always wanted to be in control," said the man after his divorce. "He decided what we would study. He didn't like my wife, so he didn't attend our wedding. But once we were married, he couldn't stop interfering. Every visit was an inspection. Eventually my wife just couldn't take it anymore. But I've never had the strength to stand up to him. His excuse was always that he just wanted the best for his children, making sure we were serving the Lord and that our lives were going well. Today I wonder if Father wasn't trying to play God in our lives."

Your role is to be a parent to your child. You are not God. This means:

- You are not the architect of your child's Dream.
- You cannot be everything to your child.
- You will never know or understand everything about your child's Dream.

❦ You will not always be there for your child.

❦ You cannot always be right.

If you are trying to play God in your children's lives, you are doing them a great disservice. Eventually, they will either bend to your every wish, becoming less than they could be, or they will rebel against you, thinking more of themselves than they ought to. Parents who try to play God are the key factor that causes children to ricochet between all and nothing. But parents who from the outset raise their children to come to know the true God open the door for them to discover that they really are somebody—unique before God.

JACOB WAS POWERLESS

Joseph's parents were absent for most of his life. His mother had died giving birth to his younger brother. His father's final recorded contribution to Joseph's formative years was criticism: "What is this dream that you have dreamed?" (Genesis 37:10). The Bible states that Jacob kept Joseph's Dream in mind, but Joseph's father wasn't there when Joseph landed in a pit. His father wasn't there when he became a slave in Egypt and then a jailbird. Jacob had been misled by the bloodstained and torn Dreamcoat his elder sons showed him after they sold Joseph into slavery.

In all the experiences that would eventually shape him into the leader he had dreamed of becoming, Joseph was fatherless. Yet he was not completely alone: *God was with Joseph.* And it was God, not Jacob, who finally brought Joseph to understand the meaning of his Dream of becoming a leader: "It was to save lives that God sent me ahead of you" (Genesis 45:5, NIV).

The harsh reality of parenthood is that often you can't be there when your children are experiencing their worst difficulties or enjoying their greatest successes. But God is always with them. The Dream Giver is the only trustworthy Guide for your children.

A teenager once noticed how his father worried himself to death, trying unsuccessfully to be everywhere and do everything to protect his child from life's difficulties. He wrote his father the following note:

> I am sure you remember, Dad, how you used to tell me stories when I was young and was afraid or insecure. Well, I have noticed that you are often worried about what might become of me when you're not there to help. Now I want to remind you of one of the stories we read together when I was little.
>
> It's the story of the rooster who got up before dawn every day to sit on the roof of the farmhouse and crow so that the sun would rise. Because that's what he really believed: that it was his responsibility to make the sun come up. He was always afraid that if he didn't crow, everything would go wrong. He kept worrying: *What would*

happen if I fell ill, or even died? How would the crops grow, and the children wake up in time for school, and the frost melt, and the flowers blossom if I weren't there to make the sun rise? The world would become cold and dark; all the grass and the trees would die and the people too eventually. . .

Then one evening, Rooster attended a party and overslept the next morning. The other animals realized that he was not there to make the sun come up and were just about to panic when they saw a glimmer of light on the horizon. . . It was the sun—rising without Rooster! He was miserable when he found out that he had nothing to do with the sun's rising every morning. And embarrassed!

But he was also extremely relieved. *What a weight off my shoulders,* he thought, *that I don't have to— I can't—make the sun come up! Yet, every morning, there it is. There must be Someone Else taking care of all this.*

Dad, you light up my life, but it really isn't your responsibility to "make the sun rise for me." I know that you know Someone Else is taking care of me.

SACRIFICING AND BLESSING

When reading the family history of the ancient patriarchs Abraham, Isaac, and Jacob, we notice two words that can help us understand how parents should react to the harsh fact that we cannot assume responsibility for our children forever and must learn instead to trust the Dream Giver with their lives.

Hebrews 11:17–21 summarizes for us: "By faith Abraham, when God tested him, offered Isaac as a *sacrifice....* By faith Isaac *blessed* Jacob and Esau in regard to their future. By faith Jacob, when he was dying, *blessed* each of Joseph's sons, and worshiped" (NIV).

Sacrificing

The account of God asking Abraham to sacrifice his son, Isaac, is surely one of the grimmest in the Bible. Yet it also illustrates a basic truth every parent needs to face: *We must surrender our children wholly and completely to God.* If you are resisting this, there are two possible reasons:

Perhaps you are trying—subconsciously—to play God in your child's life. You want to be everything to your children and always be there for them. But then you are resisting the inescapable truth that in life there must come a time when your children become independent of you (see Genesis 2:24)—and you have to let go.

You are making a god of your child and cannot imagine life without him or her. The test Abraham faced was this: Who was most important to him—Isaac or God? Your child can become your idol! To put it another way: You can be overly possessive of your child, or your child can be overly possessive of you. "Sacrificing" your child to God is to acknowledge that the two of you belong neither to yourselves or to one another—both of you belong to God.

Sacrificing allows both you and your child the freedom to follow your own Dreams in step with the Dream Giver.

Blessing

Sacrificing seems to us to be something unpleasant and blessing something good. But it is important to realize that they are simply two aspects of the same reality. Isaac blessed his sons with an eye to the future—a future he knew he would not be part of. Jacob blessed his grandchildren from his deathbed—because he would no longer be a part of their lives (Genesis 48–49). Blessing your children means:

You acknowledge your own limitations and entrust your children to the infinite love and care of God.

You understand that you will not always be there for them, but you trust in God's promise that He will be with them always. When we "sacrifice" our children, we are showing that we accept that the Dreams the Dream Giver has given them take precedence over our Dreams for them. This frees us to let them go, even if their Dreams should take them away from us forever. We have to do this, even if it means longing for them, like Jacob did.

When we bless our children, it is partly because we recognize the uniqueness of their Dreams. As Jacob said when he blessed his children and grandchildren (Genesis 48–49), we need to tell each of our children, *"You will. . ."* But we must accept that we might not be there to see their Dreams come true. If and when they will fulfill their Dreams is between them and the Dream Giver, so we should not bind them to ourselves, but to Him.

Some parents are willing to let their children go without blessing them. They are too selfish to share actively in their children's lives and quite simply can't be bothered with their Dreams or their relationship with the Dream Giver. Such parents actually throw their children away rather than sacrifice them.

Then there are parents who try to bless their children without sacrificing them. These parents want to be good to their children but just can't face the risk of letting them go. But parents who don't give their children into the hands of the Dream Giver are standing between them and the true fulfillment of their Dreams.

SACRIFICING AS WELL AS BLESSING ARE PAINFUL

Make no mistake: Neither sacrificing nor blessing is easy. The heartache of a parent who has to let go of a child could be as intense as Jacob's grief (Genesis 37:34). Often it seems easier to cling to a child for all you're worth. But that will bring far more painful consequences in the long run. You will have prevented your child from living independently, and you will have seized the role the Dream Giver should play in his or her life. Children need to learn that they cannot always rely on Mom and Dad to put things right. Only God can lead them through some of the "dark valleys" in life (Psalm 23). Even parents who have taught their children everything they can about God can't build a personal relationship between them and God.

Some roads only God can walk with your child. Some Dreams only God can help your child fulfill. Therefore give yourself, as well as your Dream for your child, daily into the Dream Giver's hands. In *The Dream Giver,* I explain how important it is to give up your Dream to God whenever He asks you to. That is what faith is: trusting God even when He demands the unthinkable.

Every day, place your children and their Dreams safely in the Dream Giver's hands. Trust God with your children. Children are extremely sensitive to anxiety in a parent—if you are looking insecure and unhappy about their future, they will feel the same. This will make them feel not up to taking the risks the Dream Giver will demand of them, which reminds me of a legend. . .

One sunny day, two paper dolls, Mrs. Pure White and Mrs. Spotless, were watching their two beautiful daughters. "Just look at Little Pure," said her mother proudly, "the whitest, most pristine piece of paper I have ever seen, if I do say so myself. I will never allow a speck of color or a splatter of dirt to spoil her beauty."

"And isn't my Little Spotless beautifully clean, too? Just see how wonderfully white she is. Not the slightest trace of a spot on her."

"Oh, yes," sighed Mrs. Pure White happily, "so far we've definitely succeeded in protecting our girls from the deceptive shades and shadows of Life."

"But who is that over there?" asked Mrs. Spotless, shading her eyes with her hand. The figure approaching them was carrying a palette and paintbrushes. By then the two paper friends had noticed the soft, dreamy look in his eyes.

"You don't think he might want to. . .*paint* on our girls?" asked Mrs. Pure White anxiously. Mrs. Spotless noticed the way he was looking at their daughters. "It looks like that's exactly what he wants to do. . ."

"There is absolutely no way I will allow this," sputtered Mrs. Pure White. "No artist is going to desecrate my child's purity and beauty—not as long as I can prevent it."

"But what if he's a Master Artist?" Mrs. Spotless asked. "What if he could create a masterpiece out of our children's beautiful, unspoiled. . .emptiness?"

"Mmm. . .but, on the other hand, he could make a hopeless mess of everything. No, I just couldn't take that risk. I'm going to make sure my child remains Pure White until the day I die."

And so it came about that when the Artist asked the two mothers for permission to draw his Dream on their daughters, Mrs. Pure White flatly refused. She took her daughter and fled into the woods. The poor girl remained there, dried out and colorless, until, drenched by the rain and blown about in the wind, she once again was reduced to pulp.

Hesitantly, Mrs. Spotless looked up at the Artist and

said, "I entrust my daughter to your hands." And Little
Spotless smiled at her mother before putting her hand
into that of the Master Artist. He painted on her a work
in flaming color—a unique version of his Dream for her.
And in the years that followed, many people came to look
at this painting and rediscovered in the depths of its
beauty their own forgotten Dreams.[8]

How Do I Teach My Children to Trust the Dream Giver as Their Only Guide?

There are a few things you as a parent can do:

*Be honest about your limitations and everything you don't
understand.* If you make yourself out to be God in your
children's lives—the one with all the answers who can
handle anything—you are putting yourself between them
and God. Your honesty about your limitations will help
your child to trust in the Dream Giver instead and seek
His direction.

*Understand that your children's relationship with the Dream
Giver is more important than their relationship with you.* Initially,
children come to know God through their parents. But
gradually you should retreat more and more into the
background, allowing them to build their own
relationship with the Dream Giver. Your child needs to
know that life will go on without you!

*Allow your children to start building their own worlds—and learn
to respect their boundaries.* While children are small, they live

entirely in their parents' world. Most parents meet the temptation to keep them there permanently. But as children grow older, they come to live more and more in a world that their parents are not really part of. They establish their own circle of friends. They start school (and are often quite different people there than the ones you know at home!). Then they move out and get a job. They might marry and start their own families. You move increasingly from a position in the heart of their world to someone standing (hopefully still welcome and loved) on the perimeter. Tell yourself: *This is how it should be.* It would be a mistake to let your children live in their own world too soon, but it is just as great an error not to allow them to build their own world. Remember, God is with your child—also in a world that to you might be alien and unknown.

Once you and your children have achieved clarity about the Dreams the Dream Giver has woven into their lives, bless them by discussing their Dreams with them and helping them see that these Dreams are connected to God's promises. You can continue doing this until the day you die. Over the years, keep talking to them about their Dreams. Be demonstrative; hug them often; help them draw word pictures of the future the Dream Giver could be planning for them. Teach them to trust in God's promise to realize His Dream for each one of us.

Sacrifice and *bless* your child—it is difficult, but in the end it will be more than worth the effort!

SECRET NUMBER 7:
REMIND

REMIND your children that following a
Big Dream requires *perseverance*, tenacity,
and creative problem solving.

*No one would ever have crossed the ocean if it were
possible to get off a ship in the middle of a storm.*
CHARLES F. KETTERING

*If Columbus had turned around, nobody could have blamed him.
But if he actually had, nobody would have remembered him.*
BENJAMIN FRANKLIN

∽

Never give up hope. Never, never, never!
Neither in the big things, nor the small ones.
And if you give in, let it be only on the basis of
principles or common sense.
WINSTON CHURCHILL

∽

The great purpose of living is to do deeds that will outlive you.
WILLIAM JAMES

"Life is strange," he said. "My parents brought me up to be tough enough to handle life, but life has actually treated me kindly. They taught me to work hard, persevere, and save. But I quickly rose to the top in my profession, and for the most part I have lived well. So I decided not to be as strict with my children. I enjoyed spoiling them like my parents could not or would not. Children need to play, I believed. Their days of work and worry would come soon enough. Now my children plod along in a difficult world. They struggle to find work, and when they do, they cannot hold on to it. They resign at the drop of a hat. They are always asking me for money. . . . It seems to me I was brought up strictly and found the world a fairly kind place, but my children were brought up too coddled and now find the world a tough place."

There is one thing we *must* teach our children: *Life is difficult*. They need to know that no Dream comes true by itself. And the fact that their Dream is a gift from the Dream Giver doesn't imply that their Dream Journey will be an easy ride!

It seemed such a simple statement when I first read the beginning of M. Scott Peck's well-known book *The Road Less Traveled*: "Life is difficult." But great truths usually require few words. This opening sentence is just such a truth.

Once a person has accepted that life is difficult, he or she stops being quite so upset by it and becoming disillusioned every time he or she discovers it anew. You'll do well, therefore, to start preparing your children for this truth of life as early as possible.

The Bible also makes no secret of it. John 16:33 states, "In this world you will have trouble" (NIV). Thank God, encouragement follows directly: "But take heart! I have overcome the world."

Out of the Well into Slavery, and Then to Jail

We do not know if Jacob prepared Joseph for life's difficulties. But we do know that Jacob's own life was never easy. He was his mother's favorite, but his father preferred his brother, Esau. After fleeing from his brother, he never saw his parents again and made his home with his uncle Laban—not an easy man to live with or an honest man. Not long after Jacob married both of Laban's daughters, he had to steal away again, this time with his family and possessions. And there was tension between his two wives, as well as among his children. His beloved Rachel, Joseph's mother, died while giving birth to Benjamin. And Jacob spent the greater part of his old age under the heartrending false impression that wild animals had killed the apple of his eye.

Maybe Jacob tried teaching Joseph some of the tough lessons life had taught *him*. Maybe the bright Dreamcoat was an attempt to protect his favorite from life's harsh realities. Many parents who have suffered themselves try to make life better and easier for their children.

I know of a girl who dreamed of becoming a cheerleader but was not selected. Her mother actually bought her a car to "comfort" her and kept her at home during the game she would have cheered in "to spare her feelings." *And* she booked some treatments at a health spa "to help the girl feel better." I wonder what will happen when one day this girl has to handle the disappointments and crises of the adult world herself—her mother can't *always* be there to sugarcoat life's bitter pills.

Both Jacob and Joseph's stories illustrate the necessity for parents to teach their children that Big Dreams demand great perseverance. Even though Joseph's life turned out well in the end, he had had an extremely difficult journey. For many years, his Dreamcoat must have seemed a mocking reminder. His Dream had begun so well, but where did he end up? Trapped in a well while his brothers decided whether to kill him. While on his way to Egypt as a slave, his brothers tore the Dreamcoat to shreds and smeared it with blood. A slave in a strange household while his father was inconsolable. Innocently in jail and forgotten by those he helped who could have helped him.

No doubt about it, life is difficult. Even when Joseph's Dream at last came true completely, with his brothers bowing before him, things still weren't easy. For how could he and his brothers reconcile after the dreadful wrong they had done to him? Even after Joseph had forgiven them and saved their lives, they still wouldn't trust him fully. At the end of the story, the brothers were still brooding, "What if Joseph holds a grudge against us and pays us back for all the wrongs we did to him?" (Genesis 50:15, NIV). This is part of what makes life difficult—relationships break down, often beyond perfect repair.

THIS SIDE OF EDEN

Parents often long to re-create something of the "Paradise Lost" in their children's lives:

- We try to keep unpleasant realities away from them.
- We intervene immediately when they are having difficulties and try to solve their problems for them.
- We move in when they have problems relating to others (friends, teachers, etc.) and take it for granted that they are in the right and the other party in the wrong.

❧ We remove them too quickly from situations they
dislike (a child who is not enjoying one school
sometimes is moved several times in search of
perfection).

Parents who do this are giving their children
(probably unintentionally) a clear message: Life is meant
to be easy and fun. Whenever you experience
unpleasantness, Mom and Dad will intervene to try to
make life easy and fun. All you have to do is complain and
the good things in life will fall into your lap.

So the false notion grows that discomfort and
unpleasant feelings must be avoided at all costs. This
promotes the modern idolization of "feeling good" and
creates a false impression of what life is really like.

You aren't doing your children a favor by fostering
this attitude. If you want them to learn the art of
perseverance—and they will need it for living their
Dreams—remember the far better approach of Harry
Emerson Fosdick's father. One morning, as he was leaving
for work, he told Harry, "When you come home from
school today, you may mow the lawn if you feel like it."
He was almost out the door when he called over his
shoulder, "And you had better feel like it!" To this day,
Harry says, he hears his father's voice whenever he has to
do something he doesn't want to. . . "And you had better
feel like it!"

Another great man whose father taught him the
principle of perseverance is Konrad Adenauer, former

Chancellor of West Germany. His father advised him, "Keep on going until the last kilometer, and enjoy the trip!"

All parents want to spoil their children a little sometimes, and so they should. But if your children get the message that they are entitled to an easy, pleasant life, they never will be prepared for real life—life this side of Eden. Some people feel wronged because life has turned out not to be as easy as they had expected. Others just give up when life's challenges become a little tough. And there are parents past retirement age, with children approaching middle age, who still saddle up the white horse and ride to the rescue of their "youngsters" for every tiny "crisis."

STRENGTHEN YOUR CHILDREN

No parent wants his or her children to drown in a sea of problems that are too deep for them. But as our children grow older, we should increasingly place the responsibility for handling their lives and solving their problems in their own hands. Unfortunately, many parents treat their children like the man who tried to help the butterfly in this classic story:

> A man one day picked up a caterpillar and decided to watch every step of the little creature's metamorphosis into a butterfly. Fascinated, he watched as the caterpillar spun a cocoon around

itself. Then the man began waiting excitedly to see the butterfly emerge from the cocoon.

He waited. And waited. After weeks of apparent inactivity, something moved inside the cocoon: The butterfly was in the process of escaping! By this time, the man was completely in love with the little creature, and he became concerned when he saw how the butterfly was struggling to break free from the cocoon. After a few hours, he could no longer endure watching the insect struggle, so he decided to help. With a small knife he cut the rest of the cocoon open so that the butterfly could break free quickly and easily. With bated breath, the man stood waiting for the beautiful butterfly to take off and soar in its full glory.

It did not. It fell. Its wings were not strong enough to keep it airborne. The man did not know that his well-intended meddling actually had done the butterfly no good. Nature *intended* emerging butterflies to strain against the walls of the cocoon; this process strengthens their fine wings sufficiently to carry their bodies. In the struggle to emerge, the body releases an essential fluid into the wings—enabling flight.[9]

This is exactly what we do when our children flounder on their Dream Journey. We protect them from all pain and suffering, disillusionment and disappointment.

But just as the man denied the butterfly the chance to grow strong in the process of overcoming its challenge, overprotecting our children is neither wise nor healthy—because then we deny them the opportunity to grow strong by having to deal with their own problems along the road of life and faith. For this they need certain *skills,* which you as a parent and role model can help them learn:

Teach your children to trust in the Dream Giver, come what may. Children need to learn that they can trust God to keep His promises, but they also need to learn *what* God promises. He's never promised to make everything in their lives easy and fun, but they can trust God to *be with them* in times of trouble and suffering. I know a young man with a particular aptitude for mountaineering who struggles with various learning difficulties. His whole school career has been a battle to keep up with his peers. Yet with the support of his parents and an unshakable faith in God's help and presence in his life, he is succeeding little by little in becoming educated so that he can support himself one day. To reward his perseverance, last Christmas his parents gave him a pair of designer mountaineering shoes with a card attached that said, *"For together with God you are climbing the Mount Everest of life. . ."*

Teach your children to have faith and be realistic about life. By the time your children leave home, you should have taught them how difficult life can be (without scaring them into refusing to leave the nest!). However they also should know that "in all things God works for the good of those who love him" (Romans 8:28, NIV). This simply means that at any given moment, I can lay my whole life—the good and the bad—before God and say, "God, You alone can make something worthwhile of it all!" This combination of faith and realism will teach your child that:

- *There are many things in life that we do not understand; still, life is good.* As Paul wrote in 1 Corinthians 13, much is reflected in the mirror of life that is unclear to us, yet love remains the strongest force in the world.
- We never find satisfactory answers to many problems, but we do receive the strength to live with them.
- Sometimes we feel unsafe, but God is always with us.
- Frequently we do not get what we want, but God's love is sufficient for us at such times, too.

Teach your children the skill of creative problem solving. When your children are little, it is natural for you to handle their problems for them. However, it is vital to progress as soon as possible from "Let me do it for you!" to "Come, let's do this together!" to "What do you think *you* should do about this?" It is important to give your children the opportunity to *try out* their own solutions as well as to *make mistakes* without making them feel that an unsuccessful effort is the end of the world.

Teaching your children to solve their own problems is like teaching them to walk. First you take them by the hand; then you let them go for a little bit on their own; still later you just are around in case they fall; eventually they need to cope with falling down, too.

Teach your children practical perseverance. Children have to learn that nothing worthwhile comes cheap! We achieve Big Dreams only by persisting doggedly. An anecdote from the life of Gary Player, the famous golf player, illustrates this:

> Player was leaving the course one day, dog-tired, when an overeager amateur golfer told him, "I would give anything to be able to hit a ball as well as you can!" Player's usual politeness temporarily let him down as he replied, "No, sir, I don't think you would. You would 'give anything' to be able to hit a golf ball like me *if it were easy*. But do you know what it takes? You have to get up before five every day, go out on the golf course, and hit little white balls *thousands* of times. Eventually your hands start bleeding. Then you just walk to the clubhouse, rinse off the blood, apply [bandages], and you get back on the course, hitting those balls another thousand times—with sore hands. That is what you must be prepared to give. The price of success is hard, hard work and even greater mental endurance."[10]

To teach your child how to persevere *wisely,* you need to know your child well and be finely in tune with him or her. If your daughter doesn't have much aptitude for music, doesn't really enjoy it, and is only taking it to please you (you're such a music lover!), your efforts to teach her perseverance in this field are doomed. Talk with her again about her Dreams, and encourage her to tell you what she thinks she will need to live those Dreams. Discover together with her other areas where she will have to persevere if she wants to live her Dreams. Perhaps she is dreaming of making beautiful things with her hands. Your practical help and encouragement to persevere in her chosen field will achieve far more than forcing her to spend endless hours practicing the piano, probably killing the little love she might have had for music in the first place. Letting your children take up something they enjoy is the best way of teaching them to keep at it! Once they have learned perseverance in a field for which they have a natural preference, they will be able later to apply this skill to other fields of endeavor.

A FINAL WORD

Remember that you, too, will need the very perseverance you want to instill in your children!

Let's be honest. Children are wonderful, but they can wear us out. They hurt us. Sometimes they plunge us into disappointment. And let's be honest about ourselves: We love our children, but we hurt and disappoint them as well; we tire them out or simply irritate them. Parenting is tough, but it brings unequalled satisfaction. And that in itself is a precious Dream. The day you held your child for the first time, your heart was full of Dreams about the kind of parent you were going to be. Perhaps these Dreams have faded with time. Perhaps you've adapted them as you have learned more about parenting. But I think every parent's Dream is basically: *I want to be a good parent to this child. I want to give my child a strong foundation in life.*

This Dream sometimes looks as if it will never come true. To continue pursuing it calls for endurance and perseverance. This requires absolute trust in the Dream Giver, who put your child—with his or her unique Dreams—into your hands. If you believe in Dreams and want to help your child to follow a Big Dream, one that can change the world in a big or small way, be warned that *this will demand much of you.* Yet we want to invite you: Wherever your children are today, whatever they're doing, don't give up on that Dream. *It comes from God's heart!*

NOTES

1. From Jack Canfield and Mark Victor Hansen, *Chicken Soup for the Soul* (Deerfield Beach, FL: Health Communications, 1998).

2. Retelling of story from Jack Canfield and Mark Victor Hansen, *Chicken Soup for the Soul: Living Your Dreams* (Deerfield Beach, FL: Health Communications, 2003).

3. R. Kent Hughes, *1001 Great Stories* (Wheaton, IL: Tyndale, 1998), 17.

4. Ibid., 63.

5. Retelling of story on James Dobson from Alan Loy McGinnis, *The Balanced Life* (Minneapolis: Fortress/Cape Town: Lux Verbi, 1997), 33.

6. From Simon Coupland, *A Dose of Salts* (Crowborough, East Sussex: Monarch, 1997), 143.

7. Story of Trevor Huddlestone and Desmond Tutu from Coupland, *A Dose of Salts,* 78.

8. "Pure White and Spotless" from Margaret Silf, *One Hundred Wisdom Stories from Around the World* (Oxford: Lion Publishing, 2003).

9. Editor's retelling of story about caterpillar. Original author unknown.

10. Retelling of story about Gary Player from McGinnis, *The Balanced Life,* 87.

Are You Living Your Dream?
Or Just Living Your Life?

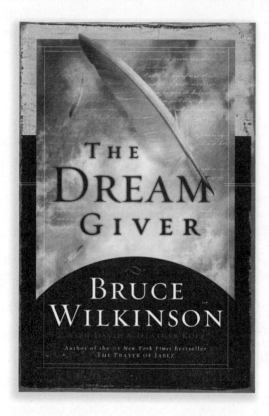

Your life dream is the key to God's greatest glory and your greatest fulfillment. There's no limit to what He can accomplish if you wholeheartedly pursue your created purpose! Let Bruce Wilkinson show you how to rise above the ordinary, conquer your fears, and overcome the obstacles that keep you from living your Big Dream.

ISBN 1-59052-201-X
$16.99

THE DREAM GIVER SERIES

THE DREAM GIVER FOR COUPLES

Let Bruce and Darlene Marie Wilkinson take you on a journey that will give you hope as you discover the seven principles to experiencing the marriage you've always dreamed of.

ISBN 1-59052-460-8

THE DREAM GIVER FOR TEENS

It's time to begin the journey of your life. Let Bruce and Jessica Wilkinson help you find your dream and pursue it on a quest to discover the life you've always dreamed of.

ISBN 1-59052-459-4

THE DREAM GIVER FOR PARENTS

In this practical guide, Bruce and Darlene Marie share with you the seven secrets for guiding your children to discover and pursue their Dreams.

ISBN 1-59052-455-1